CW00969169

HEROES AND
VILLAINS

HEROES AND VILLAINS

THE GOOD, THE MAD, THE BAD AND THE UGLY

CHARLIE BRONSON
WITH TEL CURRIE

JOHN BLAKE

Published by John Blake Publishing Ltd,
3, Bramber Court, 2 Bramber Road,
London W14 9PB, England

www.blake.co.uk

First published in paperback in 2005

ISBN 184454 118 5

British Library Cataloguing-in-Publication Data:

A catalogue record for this book is available from the British Library.

Design by www.envydesign.co.uk

Printed in Great Britain by Bookmarque, Croydon

1 3 5 7 9 10 8 6 4 2

In memory of John Dillinger, the greatest bank robber
who ever lived ... RESPECT.
Charlie Bronson

To my family.
Tel Currie

Acknowledgements

SPECIAL THANKS TO both our families and to Charlie and Veronica Richardson, Freddie Foreman and Janice, Wilf Pine, all our proper friends in the North, Jimmy Andrews, the Neighbour family, Billy Cribb, 'Razor' Smith, Harry Starbuck, George Craig, Mike Gray, Scott Gale Greg Foreman and all at the Punchbowl pub in Mayfair (best pub in London), Ronnie Biggs, Joey and Julie Pyle, Mitch Pyle, Carlton Leach, Cass Pennant, Stilks, Dave Courtney, Joe Smith, Jimmy and Wally Stockin, 'Gypsy' Johnny Frankham, Charlie Breaker, Mike Gray, Mark Fish, Jacket, Kenny Noye, Cliff Fields, Laurie O'Leary, Seymour, Gary Shaw, Tina Shaw, Alfie Hutchinson, Ray Williams, Juggy, the Currie family, the Gibbs family, the Peterson family, Johnny Knight, Ronnie Knight, Billy Brindle, Johnny Nash, Dennis Arif, Bruce Reynolds, Red Menzies, Warren, Terry Sabini, Nosher Powell, Vic Dark, Terry Turbo, Steve Holdsworth, 'Big' Tony Thomas, Bernie Davies, Duchy,

Greg Steen, Lee Richardson, Jeff Mason, Liam Galvin, Mr T, Ray Mills, Tony Bowers, Andy 'Pitbull' Hunter, Terry Smith, Mike Biggs, Ian Freeman, 'Big' John Beeching and Glyn, Eira, Julie, Veronica, TB, James Ravenscroft ... and all the other 'proper' people who can't be named – you know who you are!

And a very special thanks to the main man himself – Roy 'Pretty Boy' Shaw.

When it comes to true loyal friends, Charlie Bronson has good reason to give thanks. He says, 'I've been blessed, as over my life I've met and had the best. For example, Chris Reed, Lyn Jameson, Ray Williams, Eddie Clinton, Clare and Phil Raper, Debbie Diamond, Joe Pyle, Sammy McArthy, Di Brown and Mark and Sandra Rahim, to name but a few.

'I know my lovely sister Loraine and I fell out, but even her, 'cos I love her to bits as I know she does me. My brother Mark, he does me proud; and I can't forget all the support from Clare and Tony McCullagh, Raymond Light, Stu Cheshire, Tel Currie, "Big" Tony Simpson and Alan Rayment, Stilks, Cass, Eric Mason, Eddie Richardson, Frank Fraser ... the list goes on!

'Something I'd like to put right about Frank Mitchell and Jack "The Hat" McVitie. Both these men were rock solid, both survived a really gruelling life, both respected. Both kicked black and blue, both fought their guts out and both had a violent end!

'Whatever you think of them, you have got to admire them as hard men. Frank is still an icon behind the walls, a prison legend. Jack truly was a good bloke, but both had run-ins with the twins and they copped their lot, rightly or wrongly. Frank Mitchell lives on like no other con, and I'd like to just leave it at this.

'I'd also like to say to my son Mike, stay at it and we will sort it all out later, don't let go. I'm dying for a pint with you. Box it clever, son.

'And a big thanks to my old buddy John Blake for his belief in me. He believed in me when most threw the towel in. And an even bigger thank you to Tel Currie for all his hard work. Without him there is no book. Look out for our next one which will blow your panties off!

'PS A shout to my lovely sister Loraine. Back in my life again after a four-year absence. The rainbow's back. You watch my art come alive.'

For those campaigning for Charlie's release – keep it up, folks – the work doesn't stop until Chaz is free and at home with his family. A special thanks to Peter Lewis the guv'nor of www.freebronson.com.

Contents

The Chaps at the 'Free Bronson' launch organised by Tel Currie. *Left to right*: Johhny Nash, Charlie Richardson, Charlie Breaker, Joe Pyle and Roy Shaw. Also, a 'Free Bronson' badge made especially for the campaign.

FREE BRONSON

Foreword

Charlie Richardson:

I consider both Charlie and Tel as very good friends of mine. They are both good guys and solid men. Tel sent me most of this book in its early form and, I must admit, I was very impressed. I wouldn't have agreed to write a Foreword for it without seeing the actual manuscript beforehand and, I can assure you, I never put my name to anything I don't believe in.

What impressed me most was the honesty and bravery with which this book has been written. I say this because it's extremely easy and very common for authors to balance precariously on the fence without the spine to air their own opinions; there is no such behaviour in this book. Still, if you knew Charlie or Tel, you would know that copping out was never an option.

I honestly don't know what the authorities are trying to do with Charlie Bronson. The man is not a threat to anyone but he is being treated worse than an animal. He's not a killer but he is being treated worse than sex cases and murderers of innocent people. Still, I got sentenced to 25 years for ABH which the media dubbed 'The Torture Trial', so I shouldn't be too surprised at the way Charlie is being treated.

In this book, there were even a few names that slipped my mind and it brought many memories flooding back.

All that's left for me is to say enjoy the book ... better men couldn't have written it.

Roy 'Pretty Boy' Shaw:

Both Tel Currie (or Telboy, as I call him) and Charlie Bronson are close, genuine friends of mine. I am not the sort of person who constantly has an entourage around him and I only choose to have a handful of close friends. I have always been a bit of a loner and I won't have muppets around me. Tel and Charlie are certainly my pals. Of course, I see Telboy more than I do Charlie. Both of these are strong, honest men with old-school principles and command much respect; they also respect others in return.

Charlie may have been a rascal in the past, but even then his crimes were minimal compared to the scum we have receiving far less punishment now. I am living proof that there is life after prison. I went from the dungeons of Broadmoor to becoming a successful legitimate businessman. There is no reason why Charlie Bronson cannot achieve the same. He is actually a very articulate, intelligent and creative man. An overlooked fact is that Charlie has a heart of gold and raises thousands for children's charities, but that doesn't sell papers, does it?

But Charlie is not being given a chance to prove he has changed. How can a man prove he's changed while locked in a cage 23 hours a day in solitary? How can a man prove himself without being given the opportunity to prove himself?

I have been lucky enough to read much of this book already and I was very impressed. Both Tel and Charlie know what they are on about. It is indeed a book about the 'chaps'. Finally, the truth! Enjoy.

Ronnie Biggs:

Both Tel and Charlie have given me great support since my return to England in May 2001. As you may or may not know, I have not been in the best of health but still kept as a Category A prisoner in HMP Belmarsh.

I correspond with them both on a regular basis even though now I find it difficult to write. I have read much of the book already and it is shaping up to be the only book of truth on all the chaps.

Bruce Reynolds:

Charlie Bronson is a phenomenon in the prison system today. Charlie and Tel's book will be a real eye-opener to many.

Introduction

Charlie Bronson:

From the day you're born 'til the day you die, it's your journey, nobody else's. You're free to do whatever you like, say what you like and go where you like.

Unless, of course, you end up in prison.

But it's your journey, and on your journey you're going to meet them all – the Good, the Mad, the Bad and the Ugly!

Everyone you meet is a chapter of your life; a memory, a nightmare, a mental scar, a good laugh, whatever. On my journey, I've met so many ugly, mad, bad bastards that I think the good are so few; it's why I love and respect the ones I meet. But I do love a mad one, the ugly ones are fun and the bad ... to me, they're unique.

And talking of unique, there's one person, above all others, who's stayed loyal to me throughout my life, and who's become a real-life Charlie's Angel. My number-one angel is my mother Eira. Without her love and belief in me, I'd have been long in a box with the worms. The love she directs my way is the key to my freedom; I'd be a brazen, nasty fucker without her. So I'll take the golden opportunity to thank her for making me what I am today – a man with a heart full of love. No matter what I'm portrayed as, no matter what you read in the rags or hear in your local pub, I'm really not the animal I'm labelled.

Sure, I'd punch a hole in your head as a last resort, but I'd never do anything that wasn't deserved. I should know – I've lived with the maddest, baddest, ugliest fuckers on this planet; to me, they are all part of my journey. Like it or lump it, it's my journey! I've had a bloody good ride, no brakes, and at times I never even had a fucking steering wheel.

My journey had to crash, but I crashed with dignity. It was my pal Tel Currie who came up with 'The Good, the Bad, the Mad and the Ugly'. As soon as he said it, my brain went into gear and the journey started up again.

I have known Tel for a few years but he has done more for me than some of my pals have done in 30 years! He's a nice guy with old-fashioned morals and he bridges the gap between old school and new school. But take his kindness as weakness and you will see a very different side of him. He is nobody's fool and does not suffer fools gladly either; he's certainly no fake. But Tel is not one of those muppets that goes around barking at people and pretending to be something he's not; he has the utmost respect for genuine people. He is also liked by some of the most respected men around.

It's been a real privilege working on this project with him; we have more in the pipeline that will blow your socks off ... so watch this space!

Tel always stays loyal to my freedom campaign and gains plenty of support, whether people accept it or not. I am not forgotten and will not end my days in a security kennel chewing dog biscuits ... with pals like Tel Currie, how can I?

So with Tel's input, I'm sure you're all in for a cracking read and a bloody good laugh. Strap in tight and come on our journey ... enjoy the ride.

And you'll meet some tasty characters on the way; you'll love 'em or hate 'em, that's for sure. Me, I just live under the same roof as them; to me, it's just life.

You're in for a treat! I don't half spoil you lot!

Tel Currie:

Charlie and I originally planned this book to include people we know or have known. At the risk of being called name-droppers, we didn't have to do loads of research and tenth-party interviews. We were able to cut straight to the source and to those great people we are eternally grateful. For the most part, this is the case. But we decided that to give weight to the stories of the people we know, we would include some people we didn't know, many of whom lived and were active before our time.

This volume deals solely with the UK. Of course, there are people we have left out both past and present. Some we have not included out of respect for them and their current situations (you know who you are, lads ... a big hello anyway). Those people, of course, we would have loved to have in the book and they certainly would have been included under different circumstances.

Others, like the Kray twins, we included but skimmed over

because their story has been told a hundred times. Indeed, Charlie recently had a book about the twins published.

Most of the names in this book have retired or moved on to other careers. Only a complete fool or a grass would write a *Who's Who?* of active criminals. Apart from that, many of those included are civilians with great talent or who have done things in the course of their lives worth a mention.

As for who actually goes into each category of 'The Good, the Bad, the Mad and the Ugly', we have left that up to you to decide. Different people will have different views. But it will be perfectly obvious whom Charlie and I think fit in which categories; we don't believe in sitting on the fence.

Some of our opinions in this book may seem, on the surface, a touch biased ... rubbish!

For example, the account of the Richardson 'Torture Trial' is based on fact and, as long as you approach the book with an open mind, it will all make sense.

You may find words like 'respect' and 'gentleman' used on occasion, but only where they are truly deserved ... most of the people in this book deserve the highest of accolades.

But, whatever your opinion, both Charlie and myself are confident there is something in here for everyone.

And talking of Charlie, he deserves a bit of a mention here and now. He's a good friend of mine, and we were friends before we decided on putting a book together. There was no great plan to do a book, it just sort of evolved.

As many of you will know, Charlie is currently serving a life sentence in HMP Wakefield for taking the teacher Phil Danielson hostage. Danielson was not hurt and claimed he had actually formed a bond with Charlie. Charlie at the time was getting along well in the Unit at Hull Prison. He was happy there and was told he would be staying there. But they went back on their word and announced to Charlie that he would be moved to the dreaded and hated Whitemoor Prison. Charlie took a hostage in sheer desperation as a way of protest – he couldn't exactly ring the press – it was the only way to get his point across. He was also told that Danielson had been slagging off his beloved artwork. It's not something Charlie is proud of, but it happened and Danielson was released unharmed. Of course, Charlie had to be punished ... but life?

It's all been said before, but it seems there are plenty of folk who appear to have deaf ears out there, so here's the facts again. Charlie has never killed anybody, he has never mugged anyone, raped anyone or hurt women or children. He is simply an ex-armed robber who never pulled the trigger.

Yes, he was violent when in prison but, most of the time, he was provoked, either by ten-handed prison wardens or other tough cons. He had a short fuse and wouldn't let people take liberties with him but that's how you survive in prison. You are either labelled 'violent' or a 'victim'.

You are probably thinking, Oh, here we go, the same old clichés – only amongst their own, loves their mum, does loads for charity, etc. etc. Well ... yes, that's about right, actually. Some statements have only become clichés because they are repeated over and over again. And they are only repeated over and over again because they are true! In fact, those clichés are true of many of the chaps in this book.

Unlike many of the cynics and 'throw away the key' brigade, I actually know Charlie Bronson. The Charlie I know is a man of great heart, intelligence and warmth. If he can help, he will. The amount of money he has raised for children's charities through his stunning artwork is astounding. Charlie is not some out-of-control lunatic; he can control himself as well as anyone. The difference was, in the past, he didn't particularly want to.

But for some reason best known to the faceless lawmakers, Charlie is kept 23 hours of every day locked in a cage in HMP Wakefield. He is not even being given a chance to prove himself. How can he show he has changed when he's in a cage? What happened to rehabilitation?

His visits are all behind bars, despite the fact that he has not attempted to hurt a visitor in 30 years. If you are still not convinced that's wrong, then maybe the fact that child-killer Ian Huntley has far more freedom than Charlie will. If not, you're probably a nonce yourself.

This is the main bone of contention – why are child murderers and rapists being given more freedom and luxury than an ex-armed robber who never shot anyone?

Again, if you think it's right that Charlie should get a longer sentence in worse conditions than nonces, then you yourself are bloody suspect!

Of course, Charlie should have been punished and, believe me, he has been. But when you get life for taking a hostage and letting them go without a hair out of place, and a judge gets caught with vile child porn, goes to court and gets let off completely ... something in our society is very disturbingly fucked up.

But, Chaz, don't worry, me old china ... we will get you out one day.

THE GOOD,
THE MAD,
THE BAD
AND THE UGLY

Geoff Allen

Geoff was extremely close to Ron and Reg Kray in their heyday in the 1960s. He would drive the twins about and generally look after them, but he was in no way a gofer. He was, in fact, a first-class conman and later property tycoon who bought and sold mansions.

In many ways, Geoff Allen is one of the unsung heroes in the Kray story. He was certainly closer to them and knew a lot more about their business than many of those who have publicly claimed to be top Kray men ever did. Sadly, Geoff passed away in 1992.

Jimmy Andrews

The élite of London's underworld has always respected Liverpool's Jimmy Andrews, despite the fact that he has never been a gangster or villain. He is a family relation of the late Lenny McLean and considers Charlie Richardson a father figure. In fact, Jimmy cannot speak highly enough of Charlie ... but I am yet to meet a man that can! Jimmy is also close to Freddie Foreman and, although young, is one of the very few

Jimmy Andrews

genuine friends Ronnie, Reggie and Charlie Kray could count on in their later years. Of course, many have claimed to have been close, trusted, genuine friends of the Krays, but they were mostly getting off on the reflected glory, but not Jimmy. He was one of the few who had the honour of visiting the Krays' mother Violet at Braithwaite House and refused to go to Ronnie's funeral because he didn't agree with all the sycophants. Only the true, genuine people are in this book.

Jimmy is a very talented man. At 18 years old, his good friend Ray Winstone put him in touch with his agent Lou Hammond. Jimmy is now very prominent in the film business. He will be co-starring and co-producing a new film called *Mobs* which is bound to be a scorcher, and many of Jimmy's exploits will be documented in his forthcoming book called *Scallywags*.

Jimmy Andrews knows better than most that the old-style gangsters are now extinct and the days of the best fighter and men with real bottle being top of the pile are well and truly over. He says, 'Now, courage is only £50 a gram.'

Couldn't have put it better myself. Good on you, mate.

Lord Archer

Charlie personally felt he got a bad deal. Archer was terrified in Belmarsh of getting his cherry burst. His Lordship had a few nightmares there. God saved him in Lincoln Prison as he was moved just before the riot kicked off. If he'd have been in Lincoln when that riot blew up, not even God could have saved him.

He was very 'lucky' with his sentence; he made it out by the skin of his teeth.

Even Capone had his steaks in Alcatraz, so why not our Lord Archer?

The Arifs

The Arifs – Bekir, Dennis, Dogan and Mehmet – are a very highly respected Turkish Cypriot family from South-East London. The family, although most well known for armed robbery, also owned clubs, pubs, restaurants and even a football club. The Arifs attracted loads of press attention and were dubbed 'The New Krays'. The family has been linked to deadly gang wars with rival families like the Brindles, and attacked many a Securicor van.

In November 1990, their luck ran out. They were ambushed by the waiting police as they were about to rob another security van, this time in Reigate. Kenny Baker was shot dead by the police and Mehmet Arif was wounded and received 18 years. One source said, 'The Arifs are keeping their heads down these days, but are still not to be fucked with ... they are extremely powerful.' We shall leave it there.

Kenny Baker

Kenny Baker was one of the most prolific and respected armed robbers of his era, working closely with one of the most respected families around at the time – the Arifs. In November 1990, Kenny Baker, along with Dennis and Mehmet Arif, attempted to hold up a security van in Surrey. The raid was a disaster and Kenny Baker was shot dead by Scotland Yard's PT 17 squad. 'Shoot to kill' was a phrase now being used more and more ... by both sides.

Don Barrett

Another very active armed robber from the 1970s was one Don Barrett. He worked with Bertie Smalls ... and also turned supergrass. But putting his friends in prison wasn't enough for him. He is the only one to turn supergrass ... twice!

When he finished his short stretch after his first lot of grassing, he was skint. He went grovelling to a few of the chaps who, remarkably, gave him another chance. The logic was, there is no way you could possibly turn supergrass twice. Wrong!

Barrett did the same again as soon as he was caught and put the very men who had given him a chance to get back on his feet behind bars for a very long time. Unfortunately, Don Barrett is still alive.

Honour among thieves? I don't think so.

Ian Barrie

Out of all the Kray firm, Charlie rates Ian as the most solid man he's ever known. If anyone should do a book, it should be Ian. A hard Jock from Glasgow and ex-army, Ian is just a hard-nut sort of guy but a gentleman at the same time.

He copped his life sentence at the same time as the rest of the Kray firm and he served his time like the man he is ... 20 years of it. Once he got out, he disappeared. He's one guy who can walk tall.

Ronnie Kray told Charlie years ago if he'd have had more like Ian he could have taken over the planet. He said Ian only had to look at somebody – words were not needed, one look could do it all. When Ian was collecting, everyone paid up. You'd better believe it!

Dave Barry

Dave Barry is a legend from Paddington. He was regarded as one of the best money-getters around in the golden years of the 1950s–60s. Dave also owned London clubs where all the chaps would meet, including one in the extremely tough Paddington area.

Dave Barry was a very close friend and ally of the legendary Eric Mason. Both icons remain firm friends to this day.

Timothy Bavin, Bishop of Portsmouth

Charlie says, 'I've not got a lot of time for the sky pilots (religious ministers) as I find a lot of them boring gits, and I'm sick of reading about pervert priests with altar boys. It's a big miss with me, and they walk past my door knowing it.

'But I met Timothy in Albany Jail in the 1980s. It was down to Sammy McArthy, our own British Flyweight Champion.

'Sammy copped a 15-year stretch on an armed robbery with my old pal Harry Batt. Sammy was the gym orderly in Albany (the best ever); we all loved Sammy and respected the man. He was a dream to see working out on the bag and pads; even in his fifties, he was awesome – speed, combinations, stamina ... awesome!

'The Bishop was visiting the jail, and Sammy said, "Go down and see Charlie, as he's in the Seg B Block year after year." So the Bishop got permission to come into my cell ... with an army of screws.

'It was nice to meet a real bishop; he blessed me, or knighted me, or whatever they call it, and we became good friends.

'Funny old world! It turned out he was a Lord in the House of Lords. I never even knew a bishop could be a Lord. But I suppose, with God in your corner, you can be anything you want.

'And the truth is; Timothy Bavin is a nice chap and I'm pleased to call him a friend.'

'Big' John Beeching

'Big' John from Lincolnshire is a gentle giant and has had a lot of bad luck in life. But, I am pleased to say, things are picking up a bit and, with time, John will be back on top where he belongs.

At one stage of John's life, he was rock bottom desperate and out of his canister.

'Big' John Beeching shows his unwavering support for Charlie Bronson.

To my amazement, I helped him through and so did Roy Shaw ... and we didn't even realise it.

John read my and Roy's books and it helped him and inspired him. What a bloody great feeling to know I actually helped somebody with my book.

It says it all to me in a nutshell. You can be the maddest, baddest, ugliest bastard on the planet but, deep down, we all really get a buzz out of helping others. John's wife Glyn is also a special person.

'Big' John's on the right road. If you clock him, buy the man a well-deserved pint, and toast one of life's true survivors!

Michael Biggs with Mike Gray.

Michael Biggs

Most of you will know Michael as the son of the Great Train Robber Ronnie Biggs. But Michael's continuing fight to see justice for his father and refusal to give up hope makes him a legend in his own right. Michael is a very talented musician and has even done a spot of acting.

Michael has done his father proud the his continuing fight and he has the full support of every clear-thinking person in the country. He has his own young family, yet still finds the strength, courage and sheer determination to fight for what's right, no matter how dark the road may sometimes appear. He could be forgiven for being very bitter, but not a bit of it.

Keep going, Mike, you have all our total support ... you are a true legend.

Ronnie Biggs

If Bruce Reynolds was The Prince of Thieves on The Great Train Robbery, then Ronnie was certainly the 'Odd Man Out'.

Ronnie only got into the gang because he knew a train driver. In fact, Bruce had offered Ronnie a substantial amount of money just for an introduction to the driver; he need not have been on the robbery at all. Ronnie was determined to take part, though, and he was on the firm.

During the robbery, Ronnie never set foot on the train and certainly knew nothing of the coshing of the driver Jack Mills. In fact, Ronnie merely lay on the grass verge with the back-up driver. For this, he got a sentence of 30 years! How the powers-that-be worked that out to be justice has baffled most clear-thinking people to this day. No wonder Ronnie buggered off to Brazil! Wouldn't you?

After nearly 40 years of sun, sea, sand and pina coladas, Ronnie decided to return home with his son Michael in 2001. He was arrested on the plane and taken straight to Belmarsh to complete the 30 years.

Ronnie Biggs is now an extremely sick old man. He has suffered several strokes and a suspected heart-attack. He cannot speak, moves with difficulty and is fed by tubes. Still the authorities keep him in a place like Belmarsh top-security prison ... why?

How do you draw 30 years for an unarmed robbery? I will tell you how – the Great Train Robbery was about the class system. Men with common accents robbing the Queen's mail train, that's how. Any other train and they would probably have drawn five years apiece, if that, but the class system swung into action. They paraded the train driver all over the media for maximum effect and conveniently forgot to mention that the train was well guarded. It put the toffs' noses out of joint, that's why the sentences were so heavy. Dennis Nilsen and the Yorkshire Ripper actually got less! That's what happens when you upset the toffs.

Ronnie never hurt anyone when he was a criminal; in fact, Ronnie never was a major criminal anyway. This is not justice. It's pure revenge! Revenge against a man who sat and watched a robbery, was never violent and is now a sick and suffering OAP, riddled with tubes in a top-security institution. What danger could Ronnie be to anyone? Is it too much to ask that Ronnie be allowed to spend his final days away from a stinking prison?

The authorities obviously don't realise how bad they look in the public's eyes over what they are doing to Ronnie. Maybe they are scared and a little jealous of the fact that, despite their over-the-top efforts to show 'justice' being done, Ronnie Biggs is and always will be *a legend*.

John Bindon

In November 1978, a gruesome fight broke out in the Ranelagh Yacht Club in Fulham. Johnny Darke, the leader of the South London 'Wild Bunch', was dead and actor and hard man John Bindon was not far off. Somehow, a dying Bindon was allowed to board a plane and managed to escape to Dublin. He was now wanted for murder.

But Bindon was in no condition to run, his lung had collapsed and he was losing blood. He had no choice but to give himself up and get urgent hospital treatment. Unlike Johnny Darke, Bindon had survived the fight.

At the trial, the actor Bob Hoskins was a character witness

for John Bindon. Bindon himself took the witness box and gave his best acting performance ever. He also described how he had won a medal for bravery when he dived in the Thames and rescued a man from drowning. What he didn't mention was the fact that he had pushed the man in the river in the first place!

John Bindon was acquitted of the murder of Johnny Darke.

John Bindon was one of Britain's most promising actors, having starred in films such as *Poor Cow*, *Quadrophenia*, *Get Carter* and *Performance*. But Bindon never acted the hard man; he was an exceptionally hard man for real. He had done time in prison and became friends with the legendary Frank 'The Mad Axeman' Mitchell, the Krays, Harry Haywood and Joey Pyle.

But the most famous of his admirers was none other than Princess Margaret!

Bindon would frequently holiday with HRH and entertain her. But Bindon's real love was violence and he went at it with relish and become a respected face. He was also an extremely wild man, frequently totally out of control and bordering on psychopathic.

John Bindon passed away in 1993.

Russell Bishop

Another infamous paedophile. This reptile was accused of the double murder of two ten-year-old girls in Brighton. It's another case Charlie remembers well because he was in the Seg Block at Gartree at the time of the trial and he had just had a punch-up with a nonce and got 56 days' solitary over it. Fifty-six days in a dog kennel ... and Bishop got acquitted of both murders.

A couple of years later, he popped up again after kidnapping a six-year-old girl and having his sick, subnormal way with her. It's a miracle the child lived as he left her on the Sussex Downs for dead.

Bishop got life, but Charlie reckons you have not heard the last of him; he will get parole ... and will be back on the streets. You'd better pray it's not your street.

John Bloomfield

John was one of the greatest boxing trainers Great Britain has ever produced. He and George Francis took Frank Bruno to the world heavyweight titles and worked on the unlicensed scene with 'Gypsy' Joe Smith, Jimmy Stockin and Tel Currie. John was loved and respected by all the lads he trained, bringing many youngsters from the gutter to glory. He was a great man, as well as a great trainer, and you will not find a bad word about John from anyone who had the honour of meeting him. John Bloomfield passed away in September 2004 but the legacy of this legend will live on for eternity. Rest in peace, John.

Bill Boal

This man just has to be mentioned. It's a disgrace that more people do not know his name because what happened to Bill Boal is repulsive.

Bill Boal was a friend of the Great Train Robber Roger Cordrey. When Cordrey was arrested, they hauled in Boal as well. He wasn't a criminal and the other Train Robbers, including their leader, Bruce Reynolds, had never even heard of the man.

It is now accepted by all parties that Boal was totally innocent, although an apology from the authorities is obviously not going to happen. The police, by some miracle, made him a Great Train Robber.

Bill Boal was sentenced to 24 years and died in prison of cancer. He left behind a wife and children. The authorities rant on about prisoners showing remorse, but who's got the courage to say, 'We were wrong and we are sorry' for the slow death sentence handed out to Bill Boal?

Who are the real criminals and victims in that little swept-under-the-carpet episode.

Rest in peace, Bill.

John Boys

Geordie John was in the army with Roy Shaw and they became firm friends. In fact, Roy calls John 'a real rascal'! For Roy to be impressed by your naughtiness, you really must have been something.

Countless bullying, growling sergeants were silenced by these two tearaways. John's record of form at the time was even longer than Roy's and they embarked on many a merry caper together, many of which are related by Roy himself in *Pretty Boy*.

Sean and Vincent Bradish

The Bradish brothers were extremely prolific robbers who once worked for James Doyle. Security vans, banks, building societies ... they all got the attention of the Bradish brothers, who sometimes robbed the same place more than once. They were a good professional team at their best, but Sean became increasingly violent. Sean even appeared on TV's *Most Wanted* shooting a guard. Still, they grafted and they earned well.

But, like so many, the Bradish brothers were eventually brought down, not by the police, but by one of their own gang turning grass. Steve Roberts had been on the blags with them but now he rolled over. Sean Bradish received four life sentences and Vincent copped 22 years. Roberts, of course, is on the witness-protection programme.

Ian Brady

Why didn't they just top the monster years ago?

Charlie Breaker

Charlie Breaker is another of the élite 'chaps' whom everyone holds in the highest regard. Charlie has served time in homes, YP, Borstal and prison, serving over eight years behind bars. He can certainly be considered a first-class rascal!

As a fighter, Charlie Breaker is known and respected on every level. He was a good amateur boxer but lost his licence when he kneed a copper in the balls

At the time, Charlie was in Portland Borstal and was Number One on the wing with Nicky Lambrianou, younger brother of the famous Lambrianou brothers, as his Number Two

He was also a well-respected, unlicensed and bare-knuckle fighter. On the cobbles, Charlie fought the great gypsy fighter Mark Ripley and both men became very close friends. Charlie fought and beat many other great fighters on the cobbles, too numerous to mention. He was also asked to be the 'Fair Play Man' in the classic gypsy fight between Jimmy 'On the Cobbles' Stockin and Kenny Symes. During the battle,

Charlie Breaker

one raging traveller tried to shoot Symes with a double-barrelled shotgun! Charlie wrestled the gun from him and the fight continued as if nothing had happened.

Charlie Breaker is well known on the streets of South London as an unbeaten street fighter. At 56, he is still not shy to stand up and be counted when the occasion arises. But, like all real respected men, he is not a liberty-taker or bully and is great company on social occasions.

When legendary boxing promoter Don King was in England, it was Charlie Breaker he called to look after him and his boxers. Although Mike Tyson was King's most high-profile fighter, Gerald McClellan was his favourite talking point.

Never far away from the fight game, Charlie now manages unlicensed fighters and has 15 talented lads on his books.

You can see why Charlie Breaker is highly respected by all the chaps and considered a living legend.

John Brookes

Charlie first met this muppet in Ashworth Asylum in 1984; he was in for playing about with a kid, but Charlie didn't find this out until he bumped into him ten years later.

They actually let him out but then he went and killed an old lady in a house burglary. For this, he copped life.

Then he strangled a nonce in Whitemoor called Catweazle and got a second life sentence. He then became a grass and turned QE (Queen's evidence) against a fellow inmate. Once a slag *always* a slag. Brookes is just a subnormal muppet walking a very thin line ... sooner or later he will fall.

Tommy 'The Bear' Brown

Tommy came from Tottenham and was another of the original Kray firm. In fact, he was a sort of minder to the twins, especially Reggie, who considered Tommy his closest friend and ally. Tommy was one of the very few people the Krays would listen to and even accept a telling-off from!

He was a good fighter in the ring and on the cobbles. He was known as 'The Bear' because of his sheer size and power. The most legendary story about Tommy was when the police arrested him, but, before they did ... he knocked 11 officers spark out!

In 1975, Tommy 'The Bear' Brown was in the corner of Donny 'The Bull' Adams against Roy Shaw when the pair met in Billy Smart's circus tent near Windsor. Donny Adams was knocked out brutally in seconds. 'Hard' is sometimes an overused word ... not in Tommy's case.

Peter Bryan

After being charged with murdering a geezer and frying his brain, he was remanded in custody and held in Broadmoor for psychiatric reports.

While there, he crashed in Richard Loudwell's skull, who died six weeks later.

Well, it is a nut-house ... what do you expect?

John Cannon, 'Snake Eyes'

This piece of dog filth was with Charlie in the Seg Unit at Whitemoor in 2002. Charlie recalls, 'He was three cells away from me. Fortunately for him, it's a one-door unlock and I was on a ten-screw unlock so I never got to bump into him. He was serving natural life for sex killings.

'I believe this scumbag killed plenty. Snakes like him can't control their unnatural instincts with women and girls, but with other men they are all gutless cowards! All this type do in prison is grovel and cry about their life to the pathetic, gullible psychologists.

'I heard Cannon through the cell door one day talking to the Governor. "Sir, it's cold in my cell, could I please have an extra blanket?"

'I thought, Yeah, give him an electric one and sling a bucket of water over him! I shouted to the Governor, "'Oi ... put him in with me, I'll warm the snake up ... I'll set fire to him!"'

Colin 'Car Jack'

Charlie met Colin in Wandsworth Jail back in 1975; he had copped five years for GBH. He had hit a milkman with a car jack ... Charlie says, 'I didn't ask him why. He just doesn't like milkmen, apparently!

'I never did see him again; he probably moved on to a nut-house. Strange old world.'

Micky Carroll

This guy won £10 million on the Lotto! The bloody leeches got to him, sucking him dry; he's now in jail. And they'll keep sucking him dry 'til he's on the dole.

Do yourself a favour when you get out, Micky – sell everything and jump ship! Start a new life! Flee the maggots and leeches. Otherwise you're a walking stiff; they'll wipe you out.

'Big' Albert Chapman

This book would not be complete without mentioning this man. Albert is one of the very few men that absolutely *everyone* likes. As Dave Courtney says, 'I don't care who has fallen out with who, everyone gets on with Big Albert, he's a *proper* one.'

Albert is a 6ft, rugby-playing Birmingham chap. He owns the famous nightclub The Elbow Rooms, a dog track and has his own music business. From Wilf Pine to Dave Courtney, Freddie Foreman to Charlie Richardson, they all hold 'Big' Albert in the highest regard.

George 'Taters' Chatham

George was widely believed to be the most prolific thief of the century. He has been described as 'a one-man crimewave'.

It is reckoned that George stole in total in excess of £100 million. His hauls include the theft of the Duke of Wellington's swords from The Victoria and Albert Museum, and a mail van raid in 1952 that netted £250,000, the biggest robbery of the time. Winston Churchill himself spoke out about the problem and George's friend and sometime partner in crime, Peter Scott, named him the 'Attila the Hun of the pillaging game'.

George also robbed the safe of the 'Boss of London's Underworld' Billy Hill. It was, in fact, money that Hill had stolen from George in crooked poker games. When Billy Hill said to 'Taters', 'Don't you think you are taking a liberty stealing from me?', George replied, 'Bill, you've been taking liberties all your life ... what about the money you took off me in those dodgy poker games?'

Whatever money George made, though, he gambled it all away... millions of it.

As a result, George 'Taters' Chatham was still active in his early eighties. He passed away in 1997 aged 85.

John Childs

This prick put 'Big H' Mackenney away for life. 'Big H' served 20 years only to walk out of the appeal court. Childs confessed to five murders and stuck names up. 'Big H' was dragged into it and lost 20 years of his life all because of a filthy grass.

We all hope Childs gets cancer, the prison runs out of morphine and he dies screaming.

Nobby Clarke

Charlie regards him as 'my favourite old-timer, Nobby was good, bad, mad and a little ugly – but highly dangerous!

'It was in Parkhurst he speared a con in the bathhouse. The con was like a fucking teabag, there was blood everywhere, and how the fuck he survived is beyond me. Nobby got nuttered off to Broadmoor – welcome to Bedlam!

'But even in Broadmoor, Nobby was at it again; this time he got charged with murdering a lunatic ... back to Parkhurst!

'When he arrived in 1977, he looked like a wild man – long

matted grey hair with a white beard down to his waist and long fingernails. Broadmoor had dehumanised him.

'Parkhurst was to be the last place for Nobby; he died in his bed with a mad smile on his face as if to say, "Fuck you lot, I'm out of here!" He died reading *The Godfather*, which was lying open on his chest.

'Years of stress, pain and violence. Years of despair and years of madness had caught up with him, it was time to fly over the wall.

Bernie 'Colostomy Bag'

Charlie met this dirty bastard in Rampton Asylum in the 1970s. He used to creep up on people and give his bag a squirt – what a stink!

Not much more you can say about this guy – what a load of shit!

Peter Cook, 'The Cambridge Rapist'

No, not Britain's comic genius who passed away in 1995; this one was the infamous 'Cambridge Rapist'.

Charlie bumped into him in Parkhurst in 1976 ... literally. In fact, he smashed his ugly head in with a tin mop bucket. Cook got 14 life sentences for rape, having been one of Britain's most prolific sex cases.

Cook was a fucking lunatic, and anyone who met him will confirm that, too. He used to dress up in women's clothes and make his own dresses, even in jail. He was fucking ugly as well. He was just a total joke but he truly believed he was lovely. He didn't look so lovely after Charlie had smashed him up; it wasn't a dress he needed, but plastic surgery.

Cook has now served over 30 years before he died 12 January 2004.

Sidney Cooke

It was in the 1980s that this piece of filth with his paedophile pack of monsters killed a 14-year-old boy called Jason Swift.

Charlie remembers this case well because he was in Wandsworth Jail when Cooke and a couple of others arrived. They were attacked at reception by all the cons. One of the gang called Catweazle was later murdered in Whitemoor Prison ... now that's *real* justice!

Cooke only got 16 years for Jason Swift's 'manslaughter'. He served nine years before being released. Obviously, monsters should never be released. Cooke went straight out and abused more kids. Now what does that tell you about our system? Ronnie Biggs and Charlie get life, Charlie Richardson got 19 years for GBH, the Krays got 30 years (although Reggie served 32 before dying), Roy Shaw got 18 years for a robbery in which nobody was hurt, Charlie Kray got 12 years for fuck all, Joey Pyle and Eric Mason served long sentences for obvious stitch-ups ... and child-killers get freed after nine years! If you can justify that, you are as sick as the nonces!

Finally, after more innocent children were abused, Cooke got life. No words can properly describe scum like Sidney Cooke and his band of monsters. Only they how many victims they actually claimed. We can only hope there is real special place of horror for this lot in another life. A place where children like young Jason Swift and Barry Lewis call the shots.

Have you ever considered how much of your hard-earned

cash is taken out in taxes to protect paedophiles? You are paying for their upkeep and protection ... and they cannot be cured. What they do, they think is normal. Think about it!

George Cornell

George Cornell (real name George Meyers) was actually an East Ender who lived just across the street from the Kray family home. Cornell and the Kray twins got on well in the early days. Later on, Cornell joined the Watney Street Gang, a team of hard-drinking, hard-fighting dockers who were rivals to the twins. Cornell was regarded as a very hard man. One member of the underworld recalls, 'George was a real hard bastard, he was scared of nobody, especially the Krays, whom he treated with contempt. It's a little known fact that Cornell once gave Ronnie Kray a real hiding at the George and Dragon pub. He was well built with a neck like a bull. He used to bully them badly when they were young. The twins were very wary of George. The Krays weren't scared of many men, but they were terrified of George.'

George Cornell certainly had a nasty side, especially when drunk, and he once copped a three-year stint for slashing a woman's face. Cornell met a lady called Olive from over the water in South London, married her and settled over the other side of the Thames in what Cockneys called 'Bandit Country'.

Now, he joined up with the Krays' main rivals, the Richardsons, although the rivalry seemed mostly to come from the Kray side. The Richardsons were more interested in being successful businessmen than gangsters.

Cornell was called upon to collect debts from people stupid

enough to try and steal from Charlie Richardson. There were reports of Cornell tying people up and torturing them by electrocution and using them for golf practice!

Still, there were so many lies, rubbish and sensationalism written about the so-called 'Torture Trial', it's hard to pick the facts out of the hype.

On 8 March 1966, a shoot-out took place at Mr Smith and the Witchdoctor in Catford between Eddie Richardson, Frankie Fraser, Jimmy Moody, Ron Jeffries and Harry Rawlings on one side and the Haywards, Peter Hennessy, Billy Gardner and their firm on the other. Charlie Richardson was in South Africa at the time but rushed back to try and sort the mess out.

In the ensuing 'Battle of Mr Smith's', Dickie Hart, who was a member of the Kray firm, was shot dead and Frankie Fraser and Eddie Richardson were seriously wounded with gunshot wounds. The battle spelled the end for the Richardsons.

The very next day, Cornell and Albie Woods went to visit a wounded friend of theirs

called Jimmy Andrews who was recovering in the London Hospital on Whitechapel Road. Fancying a drink, they crossed the road and popped into the Blind Beggar. The Kray firm were drinking in The Widows pub in Tapp Street at the time. The Krays' grapevine was unbelievably efficient and soon a call was put through to the twins informing them that an enemy was on their manor. The rest is well known.

'Scotch' Jack Dickson drove Ronnie Kray and Ian Barrie to the Blind Beggar. The two walked into the pub, Ian Barrie let one go in the ceiling to get people's heads down. George Cornell was sitting at the bar facing the door and saw them walk in. Albie Woods had his back to the door and didn't see them enter, he just felt someone standing behind him. Then Cornell muttered his final words: 'Look who's here ...' before Ronnie shot him straight through the forehead. Ronnie Kray always said he had an orgasm at the moment he shot him. Cornell later died in hospital.

When it was announced on the radio, the Kray firm, already celebrating, let out a huge cheer. It was the end for George Cornell and, in effect, the beginning of the end for the Kray empire. Albie Woods was called to point out the culprits in an identity parade. Ron and Reg were in line, of course, as well as two plain-clothes coppers. Albie walked straight over to the policemen and said, 'You were there ... and you ...' Ronnie and Reggie walked out free men and laughing heartily.

So why was Cornell killed? Opinions vary, even among the chaps. Ronnie Kray's own reason was that Cornell had called him a 'fat poof'. This is possible as Cornell was certainly not scared of the Krays. It seems strange that Ronnie could have shot Cornell whenever he wanted, so why did he act the very next day after most of the Richardson team had all been nicked at Mr Smith's and locked away? If he hated the Richardsons so much, why did he not shoot Charlie or Eddie? Why shoot the only remaining rival and risk life imprisonment when the Richardson firm was out of the way anyway?

Ronnie said it was revenge for Dickie Hart; few believed him. It's a well-known fact among the chaps that Cornell was *not* at Mr Smith's that night. So, either, for once, Ronnie's information network has failed him or he had rewritten history to justify Cornell's murder. Ronnie wrote, 'Guess who got away from Mr Smith's scot free? You guessed it ... that snake in the grass, Cornell.'

Charlie Richardson says, 'Rubbish, George was not there that night. If he had been there, he wouldn't have slipped away anywhere, he would have been in the thick of the action.'

The most likely explanation is that Ronnie's hatred of Cornell was still festering from when they were kids and George would knock them about. Then there was the incident at the Green Dragon. Later on, Ronnie was told to 'Fuck off' by Cornell when Ron half-demanded being cut into the extremely profitable Atlantic machines run by Eddie, Frank and Cornell. It would seem Cornell loved winding up the twins and insulting them whenever he could.

Although the Krays saw Charlie Richardson as their main rival, they had also begrudgingly developed a lot of respect for him as a businessman, as had everyone. Charlie is still respected by everyone today. They had no such respect for George Cornell.

Ronnie's adrenalin was probably pumping all that day with the news of Mr Smith's. When the call came through that he was now without a firm and on their manor – remember, Cornell was originally an East Ender and was always on the twins, manor, this was no one-off – Ronnie's blood boiled over into a frenzy and, in a matter of minutes, it was done. If Ronnie had taken a few minutes to think it over, he may have thought better of it. The killing certainly made no sense in terms of strategic underworld moves. Then again, neither did the killings of Frank Mitchell or Jack McVitie.

Charlie Richardson recalls, 'It was wrong to shoot George, he was just their sacrificial lamb. It fucked things right up for Eddie and Frank as well, because they had been nicked the night before. They were hardly going to let Eddie and Frank go because Old Bill now think there's a full-scale gang war going on with the Krays and that Eddie and Frank had started the fucking thing!'

The wall of silence that went up around the Kray firm after the Cornell killing gave them the idea that they were untouchable. Eventually, the wall started to crumble and one of those to come forward was the barmaid from the Blind Beggar who had been serving behind the bar on the night of the shooting. Her evidence helped condemn the twins to 30 years apiece. Ronnie said he would have rather hanged than been given that slow death sentence and, in a way, George Cornell had his revenge.

Bertie Coster

Bert was a talented boxer who fought for the East Ham Club. He was an ABA finalist and, by all accounts, a bit special.

Burt gave up the boxing and went on the pavement and was a good armed robber. Along with 'Mad' Frankie Fraser, Bert was one of the ringleaders of the infamous riots at Hull Prison.

Bert was nicked with Roy Shaw in Parkhurst for an alleged murder of a man after a game of football. Both men were acquitted and Roy paid tribute to Bert, saying, 'Bertie Coster stood like a man when we were nicked for murder.' Bert and Roy remain friends to this day.

Old Tom Cotton

Charlie first met Tom in Parkhurst's punishment block in the 1970s, and over the years he's probably been back to Parkhurst more than 20 times

His first stay there was in 1991, and old Tom was still there working as a screw in the block. It was like he was part of the furniture, a brick in the wall. He must be retired by now. Charlie says, 'I will always respect him as a good, fair man. He did his job and never once tried to take liberties.

'I've had some serious problems in that block over the years with them screws, but when Tom was on duty he had a way of cooling it all down. Rather than pile in with ten others kicking ten bells of shit out of one man, he would try to sort the problem out.

'Obviously, at times he couldn't change fate but he would rather have a peaceful end to a situation, where others would prefer a good kicking.

'I've been in the Strongbox many times there, and on more than one occasion Tom has gone out of his way to make my life more humane by giving me a cup of milk or a sandwich out of his own bag!

'I cut a screw there, so many screws hated me; Tom was still always decent to me. He told me once that I wasn't bad; it was the system that makes people bad. It's not an easy job being a screw at the best of times and many do a good job – but there are some who are just sadistic bastards.

'Tom always used to buy the *Daily Mirror*, and before his shift ended he'd slide it under my door and shout, "See if you can finish the crossword!"

'On another occasion, there was a new screw working on

the block and he was winding the cons up, me included, so Tom made it clear – "Pack it in or fuck off."'

That's how he was – a fair man, and a good man.

Dave Courtney OBE

Love him or hate him, you can't ignore him!

'Dodgy' Dave Courtney OBE is an ex-gangster-turned-showman, film star, director, author and tons of other things. Despite the constant cheeky monkey smile, Dave has actually been through a hellish few years. First, he was charged with perverting the course of justice (not guilty), then accused of being a grass (total bullshit), then there was a very suspect 'accident', and then his own wife, the woman he worshipped,

Tony Lambrianou, Tel Currie, Roy Shaw, Dave Courtney and Joe Pyle.

Dave Courtney and Tel Currie.

turned and tried to destroy him. She tried to pin an ABH charge on Dave but only a total fool would have believed her. Dave got 'not guilty', and very rightly so.

Of course, Dave has been a very naughty boy in the past and has done some nasty things, but all the muck that's been thrown his way over the years has been undeserved and very out of order.

Dave started out as a specialist debt collector and owner of a security firm, a type of occupation known as 'muscle for hire' or 'rent-a-clump'!

Dave has become famous over the years and this breeds a lot of jealousy. Certain non-entities have tried jumping on the anti-Courtney bandwagon in a bid to tarnish him, raise their own sad profiles and make some money in the process, but failed miserably.

If the grass stuff was true, Dave would not be welcome in the company of Joey Pyle, Roy Shaw, Freddie Foreman, Bruce Reynolds, and so on. It doesn't take a lot of working out. The odd thing is, some of those who tried attacking him in print are not welcome anywhere!

Despite a history of naughtiness, Dave Courtney first came to the public and police's attention when he was asked by Reggie Kray to take care of security at Ronnie Kray's funeral. Considering this was the biggest funeral the country had seen since Winston Churchill's, it was no easy task. Still, 'Dodgy' Dave and his troops did a fantastic job and all went smoothly. The funeral, however, brought a lot of unwanted attention from the authorities who proceeded to shut down all of Dave's legitimate operations. Then came the next stage of Dave's career – Dave Courtney, Celebrity Gangster.

'Celebrity Gangster' is, of course, a contradiction in terms but Dave Courtney makes it work. His *Audience With* live shows sell out all over the world and his film, *Hell To Pay*, is a classic! Loads of faces turn up in the film, including Roy Shaw, Joey Pyle, Charlie Breaker, Cass Pennant, Terry Turbo and Seymour Young. His books are bestsellers and bloody funny!

Dave Courtney is a natural born winner. Not many men could have gone through the hell he has in the last few years from the authorities, maggots and even the people closest to him, and come out of it all saying, 'Fuck you ... you are never going to beat me.'

Hollywood beckons for Dave Courtney OBE ... Only an idiot would bet against him.

George Craig

When it comes to respected men in the North-East of England, George Craig is up there at the top. Brought up in Sunderland's tough East End, George simply had to fight. Approved School, Borstal, prison ... George was sent to them all and fought the system in every one. And he fought it hard.

George has been described as 'a right proper handful' by other men who knew of him and his awesome reputation.

George Craig simply took no shit from nobody, no matter how mob-handed they were.

But, like most of the rascals in this book, George has a heart of gold when not dealing with those in uniform. Against all the odds, George opened the Lazarus Centre in Sunderland. This centre has helped many alcoholics and drug addicts. I wonder how many lives George and his team have saved through their work? There are certainly too many to mention by name.

The Lazarus Centre is thriving and George's book, *Mud Sticks*, with a Foreword by Charlie Richardson, is an inspiring read.

George ... keep up the good work, mate.

Bill Curbishley

They don't come much more solid than this man. Bill would admit to being a rascal in his younger days but drawing a 15-year sentence for nothing is a lot for anybody to take. Bill was sent down for a security-van raid in Dartford in 1963; it was the biggest robbery in Britain prior to the Great Train Robbery a few months later. The firm were grassed by one of their own and Roy Shaw received 18 years and Bill Curbishley 15. But as Roy Shaw says, 'It was a long time ago and I have no reason to lie about what happened. I tell you, Bill Curbishley had fuck-all to do with it. But Bill is a proper man and I can honestly say he never complained once about it ... unbelievable man.'

After his sentence was done, Bill went into music management. He went on to manage one of the greatest bands the world has ever seen ... The Who. He remains with the band to this day and is doing well. Who can deny he deserves it?

Phil Daniels

More pure British talent that has survived over 30 years in the cut-throat movie business. Only the really gifted can be successful for that long and still be going.

Phil's film credits include *Scum* and *Quadrophenia* and his TV appearances include *The Long Firm*.

There is undoubtedly much more to come from one of the UK's finest actors.

Vic Dark

Vic is an ex-armed robber from London's East End. He was known as one of the hardest men in UK prisons. He is schooled in martial arts and possesses astonishing physical and mental strength. Carlton Leach calls Vic 'The hardest, toughest man I have ever known'.

Coming from Carlton, that's really something!

Vic was Cat A all through his sentence and never once conformed to the system. In one robbery, the police and Vic were engaged in an armed car chase that could have come straight out of a movie. The police shot Vic's friend during the robbery and Vic crashed the car, slung his mate over his shoulders and rescued him!

Vic Dark is one of those rare people that nobody can say anything bad about ... and that's saying something.

'Welsh' Bernie Davies

'Welsh' Bernie was born in the rough South Wales Valleys. He comes from a long line of fighting men, his grandfather was a mountain fighter (a term used in Wales for organised bare-knuckle fights which would usually take place on a

'Welsh' Bernie Davies.

mountainside away from the prying eyes of the law). Bernie's father was also a top amateur boxer and army boxing champion.

Bernie has had plenty of fights both in and out of the ring and claims among his pals many legends of the underground fight world.

Over the years, Bernie moved from being a coalminer to running the local doors in the valley's pubs and clubs, and then working in London. Bernie admits it's been life in the fast lane since becoming friends with all the chaps in this book.

Bernie has been a very good friend to Charlie Bronson over the years, sending him martial arts books, letters and words of encouragement and attending his wedding reception at Millionaire's in Woolwich in 2001. 'Welsh' Bernie is, in short, a very popular and respected member of the firm who, once made a friend of, you can trust with your life.

Thanks for everything, Bernie, you are one of the best.

Julian Davies

Julian – or 'Juggy', as we know him – was reluctant to be included in the book but he deserves it. 'Juggy' is from the fighting town of Merthyr Tydfil in South Wales. Coming from a place like that, he really had to learn to look after himself; either that or be flattened.

'Juggy' certainly did learn to look after himself and has a stern reputation as a true fighting man. He absolutely despises bullies and what he calls 'Drug Scum', big-mouth bullies with no respect, who pick on the weak. 'Juggy' has done much damage to this type of pond life.

He is also a highly respected author and his books *Street Fighters* and *Bouncers* are real classics. You'll want more from where they came from, so get writing, Juggy, me old pal.

Taffy Davies

This evil prat bit off a woman's nipples ... why? Ask him. He got lifed off for it. Charlie met him in Parkhurst in 1976. He was just a slag, a horrible, fat piece of vermin. The good thing is, Ronnie Kray gave him a slap, knocked him spark out then trod on his face ... nice one, Ron!

George and Alan Dixon

The Dixon brothers, George and Alan, were, in the opinion of the police, the successors to the Kray twins. When the Kray firm was convicted in 1969, the police concentrated on bringing down the Dixons. They were eventually convicted for demanding money with menaces and given 12 years.

In fact, the Krays and the Dixons were very close friends and grew up together in the East End. But one incident has gone down in Kray legend. Ronnie Kray had asked – or warned – George to stay away from the Regency Club. The request was ignored. Ronnie strolled up to George, aimed a pistol at his head ... and pulled the trigger. There was a click, but the gun failed to fire and George was saved. How lucky can you get?

Later, Ronnie gave the bullet from the jammed gun, complete with indentation mark, to George as a souvenir. It's certainly a more memorable souvenir than a stick of rock or a Kiss Me Quick hat!

After that, everything was OK again and the Dixons and Krays remained friends until the end.

James Doyle, 'The Ayatollah'

James Doyle was an extremely prolific armed robber who ran his firm like a military general. He commanded with such an iron fist that he was nicknamed 'The Ayatollah'. Firm members who let him down or pissed him off were dealt with severely. He was also known as 'Mr Big', as he would plan robberies and give orders to his soldiers without setting foot in the banks, building societies or bookmakers he was blagging.

In 1995, he was caught but his escape was classic. He complained of a bad eye problem and they let him go to Moorfield's Eye Hospital in London for treatment. Once there, he went to the toilet, at which point a man stormed in with a shotgun and forced the police guard on to the floor and the handcuffs were unlocked. James Doyle was on his way!

Ronnie Easterbrook

In 1987, Ronnie Easterbrook was part of a firm who tried to pull off a wages snatch in Woolwich, South-East London. Ronnie fired shots at the police and hit one in the leg. Ronnie was then shot himself in the shoulder. Another member of the gang, Tony Ash, was shot dead by police at the scene of the crime.

At the trial, in the Cat-A lorry coming back from the Old Bailey, Ronnie tried to blast his way to freedom with a huge explosion of Semtex that buckled the lorry's roof. In fact, the explosion blew inwards and Ronnie was lucky to survive. Ronnie copped life. That's just one in literally hundreds of stories about this man; he warrants a book to himself.

Ronnie Easterbrook never settled down, he was anti-authority and fucking proud of it. His sentence was full of shit-ups (dirty protests), hunger strikes and anything else you can imagine. Still, enough is enough. Ronnie is now in Belmarsh, alongside Ronnie Biggs. Both are sick old men and in wheelchairs. Those two have surely suffered enough.

Ricky English

Another man who knows the fight game inside out is Ricky English. Ricky started boxing as a youngster and fought 100 amateur bouts and even represented England. Ricky then turned to training and has worked with many amateur, professional and unlicensed fighters.

Ricky is now a top unlicensed boxing promoter; his sanctioning body, the EBU (English Boxing Union), has over 300 registered fighters on its books. Ricky has also worked with Joey Pyle and Tel Currie in the fight game.

You can catch Ricky's unlicensed shows at Caesar's in Streatham, South London.

Ricky's new project is his new gym, The United Fight Academy, in Watford High Street, Watford.

The gym, the biggest in Europe at a staggering 15,000sq ft, is the home for anyone who wants to take up boxing, kick-boxing or any other fighting art. There is no doubt that, like everything Ricky English turns his hand to, the gym will be a huge success.

Erskine

This piece of dog muck raped and killed old people in London. He didn't care if his victims were male or female. It was Erskine who screamed for the screws to help the Yorkshire Ripper as

Charlie's pal Ian Haye was stabbing him up. Always the same, a monster will help a monster, he and the Ripper will always be friends in Broadmoor, that's how life is in a nut-house. Monsters stick together like shit to a blanket.

After this, he vanished into the protection wings, and Charlie never heard of him again. Let's hope he's dead or dying.

Why does the system keep letting these evil fuckers out to rape and kill again?

Charlie remembers when he stood on his broken foot in the exercise yard when he was recaptured. He glared into the monster's eyes and told him to fuck off before he broke the other foot. He went back to his cell like a small boy. Always the same with that lot ... cowards.

Jimmy Essex

What a tough man he was! Not the biggest of men but hell on wheels when his blood was up. Jimmy was known as a lovely fella, but upset him and you died ... literally!

On two separate occasions, two different bullies had tried having a go at Jimmy. The result? Both were stabbed to death.

The interesting thing is, as with most of the chaps in this book, things like this only ever happened when they were provoked and had liberties taken with them. It's a painful, sometimes deadly game being a bully.

Billy Evans, 'The Beast'

Charlie met 'The Beast' in Rampton Asylum back in 1978. He had raped and butchered an old lady of 78 years of age.

One day, Evans was crying about how hard it was in Rampton. Charlie said, 'You're lucky it's not Parkhurst.'

He said, 'Why?'

So Charlie said, 'Because you would last for two minutes and get a hole in your face.'

Ronnie Field

Ronnie's game was always armed robbery; he was, in fact, one of the very best 'blaggers'. In 1976, Ronnie copped 12 years for a wages robbery in Leeds. Another stretch came for a robbery in Wimbledon. Ronnie Field was an armed robber through and through. What he was *not* was a drug baron.

In 1996, Ronnie was arrested with Charlie Kray and Bobby Gould by Newcastle undercover police. The defence ran an entrapment argument. Ronnie received nine years, Bobby Gould five and Charlie Kray 12. For Charlie Kray, it was a death sentence. The sums of money and amounts of cocaine being mentioned by the prosecution would have been laughable if it wasn't so damn serious. Whether it was an elaborate plan to put away the last free Kray, while Ronnie Field and Bobby Gould just got tangled up in it, we shall never know for sure, but the total disbelief and raw shock at this very dodgy case is still felt in the underworld today. All who knew Charlie Kray will tell you with affection that he was never even a villain, let alone a drug lord.

Ronnie Field an armed robber? Yes ... but a cocaine baron? No!

Ronnie is now out and great company ... and a lot more suspicious of blokes in Dr Marten's.

John Fielding

Charlie remembers that this bastard messed up his escape plot

Ronnie Field with Tel Currie.

in 1977 from Wandsworth. He had it all sorted, perfect; ropes, hook and he was six bricks through the cell wall. Fielding was on the servery (a wing cleaner) and he looked through Charlie's spy hole as he was digging. Two minutes later, a dozen screws rushed in like a locomotive!

They wrapped Charlie up and carted him off. He lost 180 days' remission, got 56 days' punishment and was put on the E list.

When Charlie finished his 56 days' punishment, they put him back on the wing. Guess who was still there? Yeah, you guessed it!

The next day, Fielding was found bleeding to death in his cell, blood all over the floor. 'Self-inflicted', by all accounts ... bloody attention-seekers!

Charlie was moved back to solitary. Fielding had obviously made a statement. It seems whoever did it had a pillow slip over his head and socks on both hands.

Fielding had 80 stitches from his right eye to his neck ... poor thing.

You can't miss him with his scars, so, if you see him in the South London area, give him Charlie's best wishes. Charlie says, 'It may be 27 years ago, but it still feels like yesterday to me. He ripped my dream away, the grass ... I can't forget that.'

Cliff Fields

This man is one of the greatest unlicensed fighters of all time. The great Roy 'Pretty Boy' Shaw calls him 'the real Guv'nor now'; coming from Roy Shaw, that is some honour.

Cliff first boxed in the Royal Navy, blasting out all before him. He fought 35 amateur bouts, winning 30 in the first round. He was also a full-blooded heavyweight professional.

Unfortunately, Cliff suffered the most traditional of British boxers' injuries – cut eyes. If Cliff had not been prone to cuts, he could have gone all the way. But it was in the unlicensed prize ring that Cliff Fields really became a legend.

He fought an absolutely brutal 'classic' with a very tough man named Ron Redrupp and won by devastating KO.

The man at the top of the pile at this time was called Lenny McLean or 'The Guv'nor'. Cliffy actually knocked Lenny out, kicked him out of the ring, dragged him back in and kicked him out again ... Well, it was unlicensed. Plenty of elbows and headbutts, real street fighting.

Three legends in the ring, Roy Shaw, Richard 'Red' Menzies and Cliff Fields.

Cliff and Lenny McLean fought once again a few months later. It went pretty much the same way as the first fight. This time, Lenny McLean was spark out for a whole 20 minutes. Eventually, McLean got to his feet thinking he had won. That's how good Cliff Fields was.

Unfortunately, in 1984, Cliff was attacked by a group of cowards (from behind, I might add), was glassed and lost the sight of one eye. This experience drove Cliff to heavy drinking and he struggles with the bottle to this day. But he has his good friend Red Menzies on hand, and what a great pal he has been to the big man.

Recently, Tel Currie arranged emotional reunions for Cliff with his pals from the old days, Roy 'Pretty Boy' Shaw and 'Gypsy' Johnny Frankham. I think, if Lenny McLean were still with us, he would agree with Roy Shaw that Cliff Fields is, indeed, the real Guv'nor.

Mark Fish

'Mad' Mark Fish is a man whose antics are far too numerous and far too naughty to list. He is one of Dave Courtney's most trusted allies and has one of the biggest hearts on the planet.

Mark's heart is made of gold but cross him at your peril. Mark is from Scunthorpe but is always welcomed with open arms when he comes down to London. Updates on Mark's antics can be found on www.davecourtney.com. He recently had a run-in with none other than Mohammed Al Fayed when he named his shop 'Harrold's'! A few months earlier, he sent a ladder to Brendon Mcgir in HMP Belmarsh ... Don't you just love him!

Mark Fish and Stilks.

Freddie Foreman

Freddie is obviously one of the élite, which goes without saying. 'Brown Bread' Fred's criminal career is without parallel. It's sometimes wrongly reported that Fred was a 'henchman' for the Krays and that he had done things on the Krays' orders. Total bullshit! Although a friend of Ronnie, Reggie and Charlie Kray, Fred was just as powerful as they were, if not more powerful. In fact, the twins liked the idea of having Fred as an ally because it strengthened their reputation. There is absolutely no way the twins would have stayed around as long as they did without the Foreman alliance. The twins were obviously well respected on their own, but, when people knew Fred was with them, their power increased ten-fold. It's laughable that people now think Fred was an employee of the twins or anyone else for that matter. This is no disrespect to the Krays and I don't think anyone would dispute what I have written.

When Fred heard his brother George had been shot (fortunately he survived) by a man named Jimmy Evans and his accomplice Tommy 'Ginger' Marks, there could only be one option ... revenge!

Evans and Marks were walking down Cheshire Street in

The legendary Freddie Foreman with Tel Currie.

London's East End just off Vallance Road where the Krays' house, Fort Vallance, was located. They heard a voice from a passing car calling them. As they approached, the guns opened fire. 'Ginger' Marks was killed instantly but Evans ran and hid under a lorry. Marks's body was picked up off the street and bundled in the back of the car, never to be seen again. This, of course, was underworld revenge and Fred had done the avenging, although Fred wishes to this day that Evans had been taken care of, too.

This means of making people disappear deeply impressed the Krays who would ask Fred to do the same for them in the near future. Being the loyal man he is, Fred felt he owed the Krays a favour because they had helped him after the robbery that Fred was involved in, the notorious 'Battle of Bow'.

Fred was now a successful club and casino owner and was doing well. He also owned his own pub called The Prince of Wales. Things were going well for Freddie Foreman.

Then, things started going wrong ... the Krays were calling in the favours they were owed and Fred's unique brand of 'disposal' was what they wanted.

The Krays had sprung their friend Frank 'The Mad Axeman' Mitchell from Dartmoor Prison. They were hiding Mitchell in a flat in Barking, London, but he was getting out of control and making demands. Frank Mitchell was a freak of physical power and brute strength; he was a prison legend. It was clear something had to be done, as Frank was becoming a nightmare and had made the grave mistake of threatening the twins' beloved mother. In the twins' eyes, there was only one option.

In December 1966, Frank 'The Mad Axeman' Mitchell was

told a waiting van was going to take him to the country to see Ronnie Kray. Albert Donoghue led Mitchell to the back of the van. As it pulled away, two guns fired by Fred and Alfie Gerrard opened up on Mitchell, and 'The Mad Axeman' was never to be seen again.

By 1967, it was Reg Kray's turn to be completely out of control. After the suicide of his young wife Frances, Reg was in a bad way. The story of the killing of Jack 'The Hat' McVitie is well documented in countless other books about the Krays. Jack had previously done an extremely stupid thing by misbehaving in one of Fred's casinos. That time he escaped with a warning but, in October 1967, Jack's luck ran out.

He had been taken to a flat in Evering Road, Stoke Newington, London, by Tony and Chris Lambrianou. A fight broke out in the basement flat and Reggie Kray stabbed Jack to death. The Krays' parting words to the Lambrianous were, 'Get rid of that!'

McVitie's body was bundled into the back of his car and Tony Lambrianou drove it through the Rotherhithe Tunnel. At the end of the tunnel, the car ran out of petrol and was abandoned ... right on Freddie Foreman's patch.

Freddie was alerted that there was a corpse on his manor in the middle of the night while he was in bed. To say Fred didn't need this aggro was an understatement.

Fred had to go and break into the locked car, which was a wreck. Jack 'The Hat' McVitie joined Frank 'The Mad Axeman' Mitchell and Tommy 'Ginger' Marks at the bottom of the sea, out of the fishing lanes off the coast of Newhaven. This was the last time Fred was prepared to help the Krays in this way.

Fred got ten years for his part in the disposal of McVitie at the Old Bailey. Everyone, including the Krays, knew the sentence was a liberty but, as was his way, Fred did his time without complaint.

It has to be said, Freddie Foreman has been involved in most of the top naughty events over the last 40-plus years. The Krays, the Great Train Robbery, the Battle of Bow, being kidnapped in Spain and brought back fighting all the way to England, the Security Express Robbery ... the list goes on. You don't need to be told what a living legend Freddie is. If you do, read his book *Respect*.

Fred's partner Janice is also a great person and fantastic company. Fred's sons Jamie and Greg have done him proud, too. Jamie is one of Britain's finest actors and Greg owns the family pub, The Punchbowl, in upmarket Farmer Street in London W1.

Jimmy Evans, the man who should have gone swimming with 'Ginger' Marks after the shooting of Fred's brother George, recently brought out a book that was supposed to tarnish Fred's legendary reputation. What it actually did was make Evans look a bigger prat than everyone thought he was already. When you write hinting that you're not scared and challenge people with 'Sue me or see me', only to appear on the cover with half your face in darkness and with sunglasses on ... you gotta laugh!

As another well-known face found out recently, it's not wise to mess with Fred. Anyone who disputes Fred's underworld standing has got to be completely off the planet. Freddie Foreman is without parallel and is certainly 'The Man'.

Fred ... we salute you.

Jamie Foreman

Jamie is one of Britain's most talented actors. He has starred in classic British films such as *Nil By Mouth* and *Gangster Number 1*, in which his talents as an actor are evident for all to see. He was also the star of the TV hit series *The Family* alongside Martin Kemp. Jamie is one of those performers who doesn't look like he's acting, it's all natural.

At the time of writing, Jamie is in Prague filming Roman Polanski's new version of the classic *Oliver Twist* in which he plays Fagin.

Jamie will be a megastar ... you heard it here first!

George Francis

George Francis was a notorious face from South-East London. I say 'was' because he was gunned down and killed in 2003, aged 63, the victim of a contract killing.

George Francis was yet another face suspected of disposing of gold from that most famous of jobs, the Brinks Mat Bullion Robbery at Heathrow in 1983.

He had already escaped one attempt on his life in 1985. Brian Perry was another man connected with Brinks Mat who was gunned down in exactly the same way and just a few yards from where Francis was killed. Could the same man have given the orders for both killings?

It seems that both Francis and Perry may have been helping themselves to more Brinks Mat gold than they were entitled to, but were they also committing the ultimate underworld sin ... grassing?

If so, even in today's gangland, that crime still warrants a bullet in the head.

Bobby Frankham

Bobby Frankham is another gypsy fighting legend from that most respected of travelling families. Bobby was a good professional boxer but his temper got the better of him in one fight and he ended up chinning the referee!

Bobby is also a highly feared cobble fighter and is involved with the unlicensed scene, a hard man to say the least. He is now very much looked up to and admired by the new breed of fighters, travellers and gorgers (non-gypsies) alike.

The Frankham, Stockin, Smith and Brazil families really do produce real fighting men.

Bobby Frankham with Tel Currie.

'Gypsy' Johnny Frankham,
'King of the Gypsies'

They really don't come much more legendary than this man. Johnny Frankham is widely regarded as the real 'King of the Gypsies' by the travelling community and gorgers (non-gypsies) alike.

Tel is proud to call this man a real friend, saying, 'I have nothing but admiration and respect for him ... who wouldn't?'

Johnny Frankham is the former British Light-Heavyweight Champion. Anyone who was there will never forget the three all-time classic fights John fought with Chris Finnegan at the Royal Albert Hall in the 1970s.

At the time, British title fights were not the minor events they are today. In those days, they generated more interest and passionate support than the World Heavyweight Championship does these days ... real classics!

Before turning professional, John stormed through the amateur ranks and cleared up the ABAs. In between, John and his brother Sam would thrash anyone who fancied their chances, with or without gloves. The brothers had their share of bare-knuckle fights as well, always coming out on top.

'Gypsy' Johnny Frankham has fought everywhere, from fairgrounds, racetracks, fields, pubs and clubs all the way to the Royal Albert Hall and Wembley. He's been stabbed and even shot. Yet Johnny Frankham is a real gentlemen, not loud, brash or boastful, but softly spoken, extremely modest and respectful. In short, 'Gypsy' Johnny Frankham has all the qualities of a real hard man ... and a real legend.

'Mad' Frank Fraser

Charlie asks, 'Where do you start with this icon?

'I first met Frank in the block at Wandsworth back in the early 1970s. I had heard so much about the man that I had already formed a mental picture of him. In my mind, he was a giant of a man, capable of anything.

'When I met him, he was the opposite, but beneath the exterior and lack of height was a top contender for Britain's number-one madman!

'Frank is the ultimate madman in my book and I mean that with total respect – I love the man. Who else has survived what he has?

'Standing at 5ft 4in and weighing in at 11st, I rate him as the most ruthless and fearless man I have ever met. He had over 40 years of porridge. He survived the block, the cat, bread and water, years of punishment beatings, the Parkhurst riots in 1969 (which crippled him), drug control, even Broadmoor ... Frank's whole journey was mad. Don't you just love him?

'Who else could have stuck one on Albert Pierrepoint's chin in Wandsworth? Albert Pierrepoint? Never heard of him? He was Britain's number-one hangman!

'Frank saw him when Pierrepoint came into the jail to sort out yet another hanging. He ran straight over and caught him right on the button. Only an icon could have done that ... Brilliant!

'Strangely enough, it was also in Wandsworth that I last bumped into Frank in the late 1980s. He always gave me good advice and told me to box it clever and get out fast. Everyone in jail looked up to this legend, even some screws.

They were all puzzled at why they could not beat Frankie Fraser; it was a type of respect. You can't but respect an unbeatable man. They gave it to Frank a hundred times over ... and he took the lot.

'Today, Frank is over 80 years old, still as mad as ever and still the staunchest of men. Even in his seventies he survived a bullet in the head. A normal man of 70 would have died of shock, but not Frank ... he chased after the gunman! He's a fucking true-life superman.

'"Mad" Frankie Fraser? I have had 30 years of jail, I have done Broadmoor and I don't know another like Frank. Today's villains/gangsters, call them what you will, they are not fit to clean Frank's shoes, and that's no disrespect to anybody, I am just telling you there is only one Frank Fraser.

'Frank, we love you, don't ever forget it. You have been an inspiration to many and, I'm sad to say, your values and

Frank Fraser, Charlie Richardson and Tel Currie.

loyalty are a thing of the past today. All the old lags would tell you the same.

'Max respect.'

Ian 'The Machine' Freeman

Ian was already well on his way to being a legend before his autobiography, *Cage Fighter*, hit the shops in 2004.

Born in Sunderland, he lived a pretty normal life until an incident changed it for ever. He was severely beaten by a bunch of thugs after a night out and made it his mission that it would *never* happen to him again.

After a strict weight-training regime, Ian Freeman transformed himself into a fighting machine. He was working the doors at 20 years old before running them and having his own army behind him. He was fearless and quickly known around town as a man who would take on anyone without a thought to their reputation or how many of them there were. To him, it was business. With hundreds of street fights under his belt, he was a champion bodybuilder and formidable boxer when he hit another turning point.

Ian has never backed down from any challenge – in this particular fight, he was knocking seven shades out of his opponent (Ian was still recovering from a weekend on the sauce) but it seemed to be taking for ever. After dropping the guy, Ian decided that there had to be more to fighting than just boxing. This was when he took up ju-jitsu and discovered a whole new world of fighting. He worked his way up the ranks in no time at all and was winning titles left, right and centre. The fighting machine was officially crowned ... step forward Ian 'The Machine' Freeman, total fighter.

No one could touch him – not even UFC fighter Travis Fulton. This was Ian's first big fight and he *owned* Fulton from start to early finish. He got himself known in the UFC with convincing wins, and travelled the globe, twice becoming Mixed Martial Arts Champion. Fans will remember him most for his destruction of Frank Mir when the UFC came to London. First-round victory went to Ian when Mir was having difficulty convincing the ref that he was still breathing.

Ian has gone from strength to strength since then. He's now promoting his own fights in the North-East with his company Pride & Glory and was recently picked to host Sky One's tough-man challenge *Britain's Hardest*. I think that speaks for itself, don't you?

John Henry Gallegher

It was in Hull Jail in 1975 that Charlie bumped into Gallegher. He got seven years for GBH on a priest. This subhuman had evil coming out of his pores; nobody liked him in Hull. The cons all gave him a wide berth, there was just something in the way he conducted himself. He had those frog eyes, always fixed in a stare. He got a few clumps off the lads over things going missing from cells. Cons despise jail thieves.

Charlie and Gallegher had words and it was off. Charlie smashed the granny out of him and cut him up with a jug. As usual, Gallegher squealed like a pig and made a ten-page statement and Charlie got more time added on to his sentence at Hull Crown Court.

Gallegher spent the rest of his sentence on Rule 43 protection and, years later, he changed his name to Morrison.

He also killed four old people and was certified. He will spend the rest of his life in Ashworth Asylum.

The day Charlie cut him up he just knew he was evil. He turned out double evil and a filthy grass, too.

Liam Galvin

Liam is the official cameraman of the chaps. He is well liked by all of them and films all the unlicensed boxing shows, charity events and get-togethers. When the chaps want something filmed, Liam is the first man they ring. When they don't want something filmed, Liam is always in attendance as a friend.

Luke Goss

I have to admit, when I heard Luke was playing Charlie Richardson in a film, I was cynical. How could the ex-Bros star possibly play such a role convincingly?

Well, he bloody did!

His performance in the movie *Charlie* was nothing short of stunning. Luke Goss has been reborn as a first-class actor. I strongly suggest to anyone who hasn't seen the film to watch it. It can only be the start of a phenomenal career for Luke.

Mike Gray

Just as Red Menzies is indispensable to Cliffy Field, Mike Gray is indispensable and irreplaceable to Sir Ronnie Biggs.

Mike is a close personal friend of the legendary Great Train Robber and is the figurehead of the campaign to release him. When Ronnie decided to return to England in May 2001, Mike was alerted before the UK press. Mike was also present at

Ronnie's wedding in Belmarsh in 2002. An honour, indeed, as only ten guests were allowed to attend.

People like Mike, Tom and Red work tirelessly for their friends without fanfare and with little credit. In this world of sycophants, hangers-on, fame whores and reflected-glory seekers, their type is very rare and very special and that's why they deserve a mention in this book, not just the main faces.

Mike and Michael Biggs have worked together on a Free Ronnie Biggs record and Mike is one of Ronnie's very few regular visitors. Let's hope the work, determination and loyalty of people like Mike Gray pay off and the government finds the heart to release Sir Ronnie Biggs!

Mickey Green, 'The Pimpernel'

Mickey Green was a bank robber from North London until he realised the real money was in the drugs trade. But Mickey Green was no street-corner pusher, he built a global smuggling empire estimated at anywhere between £100 and £200 million!

He got his name 'The Pimpernel' because he simply could not be found. He was also connected to the American Mafia and Colombian drug cartels. While he was being flown to France to face trial, he escaped from the plane when it stopped to refuel.

Mickey Green was nearly put away by one of his own when Constantine Michael Michael squealed his head off and had loads of people put away. Mickey Green was cleared and Michael Michael was left with a price on his head.

Mickey Green remains a free man ... and he's got a few bob as well.

Brian Hall

One of the toughest men on the cobbles and the street was Brian Hall. He defeated tough men like Albert Reading and was at one time Henry Cooper's sparring partner. Brain was also Roy Shaw's sparring partner for the first-ever unlicensed fight, Roy Shaw v Donny 'The Bull' Adams. Anyone who saw those training sessions will tell you they were more blood-soaked and brutal than most of the actual real fights!

Brian is one of the nicest men you could wish to meet and, until recently, ran the Rising Sun pub in Essex.

Rocky Hart

This guy was one of 'the chaps', a well-respected man, everyone in Parkhurst liked him. He did his porridge like a good 'un.

He had a job in the kitchen (the best job in the jail), steaks every day, plenty of milk and good wages ... plus his fiddles.

Charlie recalls that it was in the mid-1980s when Big Fatso Rogers arrived at Parkhurst. 'This guy was a fucking slag. He had already killed a woman and got lifed off. Nobody spoke to him ... would you? He had that greasy, smelly look about him, like a snake in the grass.

'How the fuck did a slag like him get a job in the kitchen preparing our grub? It makes you puke to think of it.

'Rocky was the number-one meat man at the time. Rogers got in a row with him over some pork chops on one occasion, and walked off sulking, but then crept back and gave it to Rocky in the back with a big fuck-off knife.

'The whole jail almost went up that day; the cons went mad.

'Rogers later got his second life sentence and Rocky went home in a body bag.

'For what it's worth to Rocky's family, I can say to them, be proud of Rocky, 'cos he was a blinding fella, well respected by all, a proper Londoner with good qualities ... he's sorely missed.'

Dougie Hamilton

This old boy was a lovely old loony Charlie met in Broadmoor. He was another 30-years man.

Dougie was in his sixties at the time I met him, a Broadmoor veteran.

One day, the psychiatrist called him up for his monthly interview. Dougie walked in, grabbed the doctor's pen, shoved it in his mouth ... and he swallowed the fucking thing! Gulp ... gone!

Thomas Hamilton

Charlie recalls that he was in the Seg Block, awaiting trial, when he first came across 'this piece of shit who massacred all those innocent children at Dunblane. I will never forget the photo in the papers of those smiling angels in their school picture. Horrors like Dunblane stay with you for all time, they stay seared in your brain.'

How could anyone do such an evil thing? For what purpose? There can no justification for harming kids ... NONE.

Hamilton was pure evil, spineless and heartless and a fucking nobody. They are always nobodies wanting to be somebody, but they are born losers. They don't have talent and they certainly don't have what it takes to be *real* criminal faces, so they pick on children to make a name for their sad selves ... Pathetic.

Evil is evil. Forget all the psychology bullshit – 'I did it because my daddy never bought me sweets when I was little and it really disturbed me ...' – the fact is, evil is just fucking EVIL!

Thomas Hamilton was one of the most evil bastards ever to set foot on our land. He did do one good thing in his life, though ... he blew his own brains out and for that ... well done.

Danny Hansford

Danny is a top film scriptwriter, if not the best. He had to have a mention – guess who's doing Charlie's script? With Danny on board, it will explode in your head. And we'll all drink to that!

Billy Hill, Jack 'Spot' and Albert Dimes

Billy Hill was the role model and predecessor to such legends as the Krays and 'Mad' Frankie Fraser. He modelled himself on the American Mafia dons and was the self-professed 'Boss of Britain's Underworld'.

Hill took this title when he won a famous victory over the White family in 'The Battle That Never Was' in 1947, so called because the tension between Hill's gang and the Whites had risen to a crescendo before evaporating in an anti-climax with only a few of the White gang being cut and the rest doing a runner.

Billy Hill joined forces with the other major gang boss of

the era, Jack 'Spot' Comer. Jack Comer had earned the nickname 'Spot' because he was always on the spot when Jews were being attacked in the East End. He was instrumental in breaking up and attacking the fascist Oswald Mosley's marches. From there, he turned protection into his stock-in-trade and later had the prime betting pitches at the major racetracks. According to 'Spot', he made Hill what he was and brought him up from small-time operator to major player. Hill, though, thought differently, and it didn't take too long for him to feel he didn't need 'Spot' any more. Hill now had a new ally, Albert Dimes, known as 'Italian' Albert and this alliance completely isolated Jack Spot.

'Spot' was now becoming increasingly unpopular and his gang was weak and full of faces well past their gangland prime. The Hill–Dimes alliance, on the other hand, was becoming increasingly stronger with loyal soldiers like 'Mad' Frankie Fraser.

Then, in 1955, Jack 'Spot' made what many deemed to be his worst mistake and the one that led to his downfall; he attacked Albert Dimes in Frith Street, Soho, London.

Revenge was not long in coming and, in 1956, 'Spot' was virtually cut to pieces by 'Mad' Frankie Fraser, Billy Blythe, Teddy Dennis and others. He survived ... just.

This attack signalled the end of Jack 'Spot'. His and his wife's actions in the trial against his attackers did not help his case; it certainly went against the gangland code.

Now Billy Hill and Albert Dimes were left to reign supreme. Following Albert Dimes's untimely death from cancer, Billy Hill was the main man.

Billy Hill retired with his money, his health, his reputation and his freedom. Although actually employees of 'Spot', the Krays would claim Billy Hill as their role model and they his protégés. Hill died on New Year's Eve 1984. Jack 'Spot' died broke in a nursing home in 1996.

Myra Hindley

Burn, you bitch!

Steve Holdsworth

'Sir Steve', as he known by us in the fight game, is simply the best commentator/MC there is in the whole of boxing. His ability to put new fighters at ease, conduct shows in the most professional manner and make ordinary shows into real events is legendary. Steve is the boxing commentator on Eurosport and a better man they could not have for the job.

Richy 'Crazy Horse' Horsley

This man is one of the most well-known and renowned fighters in Britain today. He was a good amateur but built his reputation mostly in bloody and brutal street battles. Richy's account of his activities on the cobbles can be read in his book *On the Chin*.

In July 2003, 'Crazy Horse' was persuaded into the unlicensed ring by Tel Currie and topped the bill at the first of the legendary 'Warriors' shows at the Hammersmith Palais, London, in July 2003. Richy destroyed his opponent in the very first round with sickening body shots that would have felled an elephant. But it was in his next unlicensed fight against Gary Marcel on the second 'Warriors' show that

'Sir' Steve Holdsworth.

Richy earned the respect of everyone in the game. Three rounds of one of the most bloody and brutal unlicensed fights in recent memory showed the raw, fighting heart of both men. Richy lost that battle on points but won many admirers with his courage and conduct after the fight.

At this point, we must mention that Richy's beloved mother passed away in the summer of 2004. She was a wonderful lady and shall be missed.

But the best of 'Crazy Horse' could be yet to come. Richy has challenged a man who is currently serving time in HMP Wakefield to a fight when he is released. Of course, the man has accepted and would love to get it on with 'Crazy Horse'. The man's name is ... Charles Bronson.

Billy Howard, 'The Soho Don'

Billy Howard was a South London boy who went on to become one of the most powerful men in London's underworld in the 1960s. The Kray twins looked up to him and admired him greatly. He wore dapper suits and was a real gentleman. He was also one of the most deadly bare-knuckle street fighters London has ever seen.

Billy ran his own lucrative protection racket in London's Soho. He also ran his own nightclubs and made a fortune from gambling. The punishment Billy dished out to anyone stupid enough to cross him was legendary, and he was well known for his talents with a knife.

Billy Howard was not keen on being in the limelight like the twins, but his power and hold over Soho was beyond doubt. You don't get named 'The Soho Don' for nothing.

Andy 'Pitbull' Hunter

Andy is the nicest person in the world and a real odds beater. Andy was overweight, diabetic and had never boxed in his life until he employed Tel Currie to train him in 2001. Andy lost stones in weight, his diabetes disappeared and he became one of the hottest properties on the unlicensed scene. His very first fight with Tel in his corner was against ex-pro 'Mad' Mickey Harrison, and what a fight it was! The small crowd of mainly gypsy fighting men who witnessed that encounter will tell you it was one of the most exciting ever. It had everything you would expect from the prize ring and much more. The referee, 'Gypsy' Joe Smith, could not split the two men at the end and a blood-soaked draw was declared. Like the real warriors of days of old, Andy and Mickey celebrated together after the fight and remain firm friends. It must also be said that 'Mad' Mickey Harrison is also very highly thought of. He is unbeaten in his unlicensed career.

Andy's career as an unlicensed fighter is now over, but the excitement of seeing the 'Pitbull' in action lingers on.

Niza Hussain

It was in the early 1970s that Niza and his elder brother Arthur both got life over the murder of Muriel McKay. But the body was never found. It's one of the rare murder cases in which the victim's body remained undiscovered.

Charlie met Niza in Parkhurst in '76 and he met Arthur in Ashworth Asylum in '84. He used to say to them, 'Come on, did you put her in a curry?' They just used to laugh and say, 'No.'

Charlie thought they fed her to the pigs because they had a pig farm, and pigs will eat anything.

Niza was only 18 years old when he got life; Arthur was older, pushing 30 years old. But Arthur lost the plot and went mad, while Niza just plodded on and did his time easy. He could make a wicked curry ... the best in Parkhurst!

The last Charlie heard of him, he got released in the early '90s and went back home to Trinidad. He served 20 years and still never said where the body was ... or did he even know?

Had they even done it? If they had, they must have been very strange to keep it a secret so long.

Charlie says, 'I'll always stick up for Niza's curries ... he was the dog's bollocks. But, I must admit, when I used to share a meal with him, I often used to imagine them eating Muriel! Then, at the end of the day, just when I was about to fall asleep, I'd think ... nah, it was the pigs!'

Alfie Hutchinson

Alfie was a very, very good amateur boxer; he even fought the legendary Dick McTaggart. Later, Alfie became a first-class rascal and did his bit behind the wall. Alfie built up a solid friendship with Roy Shaw which continues to this day. In Roy's words, 'Alfie was up front, said what he had to say and fuck the rest!'

Alfie Hutchinson is well liked and respected by everyone ... a living legend.

Max Iacovou

Max is one of the most respected doormen in the UK. He is a gentleman and his ways are of the old school.

On the door, Max is quick to respond to any incident and what this man lacks in physical size he more than makes up for in heart. An astute businessman, he makes a mockery of the old idea of bouncers being mindless thugs. If there was ever living proof of the saying 'it's not the dog in the fight but the fight in the dog', Max Iacovou is that proof.

Max was born in the mainly Greek community of Hornsey, North London, in the 1960s. As kids, both Max and his brother seemed always to be getting into trouble, both with other kids and the police. By this time, the Iacovou family had moved to Peckham, South-East London. After getting into ever more serious trouble, Max's father moved the family to Kent. By this time, Max had become involved in the security business, working with big skinhead bands of the day like Bad Manners.

At the age of 21, Max met a guy called Stilks at Pecs Gym. Stilks knew Max had worked the doors and had heard of his growing reputation. Stilks asked Max if he wanted to work with him at the Station Hotel in Welling and Max accepted. The Station Hotel was an extremely troublesome place to keep order in and, on Max's third night, things went from bad to worse.

'I refused a person who was not of the correct dress code and thought no more about it. As we left the club that evening, we realised we were being followed by a car, then suddenly the car span off. I had my mate Mr J with me in the passenger seat. As I was driving down a hill, I saw the guy who was following us aiming a shooter. I said, "Fuck me, Mr J, he's got a gun!" His reply was, "Fuck him! Pull over ... I'll get the cunt!"

'There was no way I was stopping, but Mr J wanted to get out and have it; I didn't listen and carried on driving. To my disbelief, Mr J opened the door and went to hit the guy. The guy was completely shocked at this and dropped the shooter, found his feet and ran away!'

Soon, Max and Stilks had formed a good friendship and a tight and trusted working relationship on many doors together. Stilks appointed Max as head doorman at the Squire in Catford and, again, it was a clear-out job. This was some task as the pub had about 350 people and 200 of them were trouble.

'We had this one bloke who came in called Arthur who was a proper crank. He was 6ft 4in, big scar down his face, and would dress in full Nazi uniform. He used to go behind the bar and help himself. I went in and told him to get out from behind the bar. He replied he was a barman so I shouted back, "Get out of the fucking bar!"

'After Arthur went outside, he wanted to fight all six doormen. I said, "You can fight me, mate, I'm the smallest." He then went on about all the nasty things he had done and all the people he had hurt. I snarled, "So fucking what? Are you going to have it or what?" He decided not to. This confrontation with a true headcase gave me ample respect.'

Max has seen noses bitten off, bones broken, ears cut off with axes and all manner of other extreme violence you can name. Yet, he remains a true gent and very anti-bully. When Max and Stilks team up to work, a more professional team is impossible to find.

'I have learned that, no matter what the situation, *never back down*! That way, you get your respect because, at the end of the day, everybody bleeds and has weakness.'

One thing Max has from others, without doubt, is respect.

George Ince

George Ince just has to have an entry, because he did the unthinkable – he got it on with another con's wife!

You simply do not do that sort of thing. And of all the people to do it to, he did it to Charlie Kray! Can it get any more out of order? Charlie was loved and respected by everyone, I don't think he had a single enemy. Charlie was a one-off, a very special person ... not that that stopped Ince. Sure, it takes two to tango but Ince made the move on Dolly Kray and he paid the price for it ... a shotgun down his trousers!

Then, later on, he ended up in jail and got his face sliced open. Let it be a lesson to those who cannot keep themselves under control; do not take liberties with cons' wives.

Any man who sniffs after a jailbird's wife is a no-good, evil bastard.

There are plenty of single ladies out there, so there is no excuse.

Johnny Jacket

Johnny Jacket

Johnny Jacket – or simply 'Jacket' – is well known and respected among the chaps. 'Jacket' (real name Michael Santry) was born in West London and turned to crime at an early age. He later moved up the criminal ladder and was a prolific armed robber and baron. 'Jacket' spent many years behind bars and, as a result, has now been out of crime for over five years and is a proud father.

He became a close and trusted friend of Reg Kray and was with him during his final days in Wayland Prison. He was also a key member of Dave Courtney's security firm, which, among many other jobs, took charge of security at Ronnie Kray's funeral. 'Jacket' shares his time between West London and his closest pal Dave Courtney's home in Plumstead, South-East London. 'Jacket' is currently working on his own book, which will be a real winner.

Bill Kelly, 'Mr T'

Known as 'Mr T' by all the chaps (for obvious reasons), Bill Kelly is one of our most respected fighting men. Ask Cass Pennant who he would want by his side in a ruck, and he will instantly tell you 'Mr T'.

'Mr T' ran away from home at 14 years of age and joined the travelling fairs. For 'Mr T', the natural progression was to the boxing booths where he fought all-comers and was soon having serious side bets laid on him. This led to the legendary bare-knuckle battlefields of Epsom Racecourse and Appleby Fare. 'T' recalls, 'It was unusual for a young black cunt like me to keep bowling them over like I did.' Eventually, this led to the most notorious bare-knuckle hot-bed of all ... Ireland.

'Mr T' was taken under the wing of a man named Jock Simms who saw his potential as a brawler. Simms thought 'T' was blessed and gave him some advice he remembers to this day: 'The race in life is not for the swift, it's for the ones who can endure it.'

'Mr T' was soon fighting in Waterford on farms, in backs of pubs and barnyards, packing the house every time. 'T' recalls, 'I remember once fighting this really tough Irish guy, he would just not go down, he just kept coming back like a bad penny. I really had to dig deep for that one, in the trenches stuff. This tear-up went on for about 45 minutes. This man was 5ft 4in but what a game cunt he was. It's not about physical size in this game, it's about a man's heart. You see a man's face but not his heart. I will always have fond memories of Ireland, because, believe me, this is one black cunt who fought the best of them.

'Life has taken me on some incredible journeys. Here's some advice for all you would-be fighters out there: the fight game is not an easy game. You have to have plenty of balls and plenty of heart. This generation coming up really don't give a fuck about "straighteners", it's all about the snub-nose .38 revolver. It's about million per cent results. Also, remember – bullies *always* come unstuck ... so don't be a mug!'

Advice from a true fighter and true gentleman ... you would do well to take it.

Johnny Knight

Charlie met John in Gartree in the late '80s; he's the brother of Ronnie Knight, Barbara Windsor's ex-husband.

John was a blinding cook, if not the best! One day he was doing a steak; you could smell it all over the wing, and it smelled delicious. He would shout out of the TV room to turn it over, make sure it was all sweet, sort the spuds, etc.

Harry Johnson, or 'Hate 'Em All Harry', was also on the wing. Now Harry is just Harry.

He was cooking up one of his stews and he just fancied John's steak – so he put it in his stew – simple as that.

John came back out to see how his steak was cooking ... and the rest is history. Fucking hell, John went mad! Well, who wouldn't? But Harry just stirred his stew and said to John, 'This shit-hole is full of thieves!' Obviously! John didn't know at this time that his steak was in Harry's stew.

It was only some weeks later that Harry was found in the shower with a serious lump on the head. That's Harry for you, nothing new to him!

Looking back on incidents like that can only make you smile. John served 14 years of his 22-year stretch and ended up living just outside Charlie's home town of Luton.

His wife stood solid all the way through. A couple of years back, he sent Charlie a signed copy of his book, and what a fucking good read it was, too.

Good luck, John. Box it clever!

Ronnie Knight

Ronnie Knight and the Krays were probably the original gangster celebs. Now Dave Courtney is known as gangster celeb number 1 but Ronnie was a household name years ago. Even though he never set out to be a 'celeb' the press loved him. Ronnie had it all, money, a beautiful and famous wife in Barbara Windsor, designer suits and his own night club the A & R club in London. Some younger readers may remember when Ronnie Biggs returned to England, but don't remember the fuss that was made when Ronnie Knight returned from Spain. Let me tell you, it was huge news! I actually think a bigger deal was made of Knighty coming home than Sir Ronnie Biggs. At the height of what the press called the Costa Del Crime the two same names always popped up as the kings of the Costa, Ronnie Knight and Freddie Foreman.

Ronnie and his brothers grew up with the Krays in Bethnal Green but the Knights' style was based more on brains than the muscle the twins always relied upon. Ronnie's business partner in many ventures was Micky Regan. Micky was also a close friend of Freddie Foreman and is a legend in his own right with a spotless reputation and he deserves a massive gee (compliment) here. In 1970, the youngest Knight brother was stabbed to death by Alfredo 'Italian Tony' Zomparelli. Zomparelli got bird for the attack but was out in 1974. He should have stayed in because he was soon shot dead in an amusement arcade in Soho.

Ronnie and Nicky Gerrard, the son of Alfie Gerrard, were arrested but cleared of the murder at the Old Bailey. Barbara Windsor (Who is loved by all the 'chaps' as 'one of your own') made an appearance at the trial as a character witness for Ronnie. The surviving Knight brothers Ronnie, Johnny and Jimmy never got over losing their youngest brother.

On 4 April, 1983, the biggest cash robbery in British history at the time took place, the Security Express robbery. Ronnie's brother Johnny was the mastermind behind this legendary job. Johnny received an outrageous 22 years at the Old Bailey. Ronnie himself came home to face the music in 1995 and got seven years for handling cash from the robbery.

Freddie Foreman was literally dragged back to England. (It's said Fred's teeth marks are still in a wooden door where he bit into to stop them forcing him onto the plane... Nobody can say Fred did not put up a fight.)

Ronnie Knight now lives peacefully near Cambridge and doesn't put himself on show much but his reputation as a legend is more than secured, he's an icon. Charlie is proud to say Ronnie is a friend and a fantastic bloke. When Charlie told him he was the first 'celeb gangster' he answered with typical modesty, 'Leave off mate.'

If you like books to take you on a rollercoaster journey, Charlie strongly suggests you read Ronnie's *Blood and Revenge, Living Dangerously* and Ronnie and Johnny Knight's *Gotcha! The True Story of Security Express*.

Ronnie. Tel and Chaz love ya, mate, be lucky.

Charlie Kray

This man was one of the most loved legends among 'the chaps' and certainly one of the most sorely missed. But – surprise, surprise – there are scumbags now writing books slagging even Charlie off. Funny thing is, the low-lifes who slag off respected people are always nobodies and a bit of a joke. Ask anyone who is respected and they will tell you about the real Charlie Kray.

For those who don't know, Charlie was the eldest brother of the Kray twins Ronnie and Reggie. It was actually Charlie who taught the twins to box and all three brothers went on to become good professionals.

Charlie was less criminally ambitious than his younger brothers and was more of a wheeler and dealer. He did show

Kray Corner at Chingford Mount Cemetery.

a flair for business in the early days, though, and he and Reg, especially, built up the Kray club empire. It was actually Charlie Kray who was friends with Freddie Foreman first and not the twins; they met Freddie through Charlie.

The twins were out of control by the end, but serious liberties were being taken with Charlie Kray that would go on for the rest of his life. When Reg killed Jack 'The Hat' McVitie in 1967, Charlie Kray was in bed and knew nothing about it; he was never really a member of the 'firm', Charlie did his own thing. So how the hell did Charlie Kray get ten years for being an accessory to murder in the McVitie case? Ten fucking years for being in bed and having the surname Kray!

Freddie Foreman also got ten years after the car containing McVitie's corpse was dumped on his doorstep.

It's obvious how the police were thinking – even though Charlie was never a dangerous villain or a threat to anyone, his name was Kray and, therefore, he had to go.

Charlie served his time without complaint like the man he was and, upon release, wrote his memoirs *Me and My Brothers*.

Charlie was very much his own man and fell out with his brothers on numerous occasions, not least over the script of the film *The Krays*, on which he was an adviser. Needless to say, the twins hated the film and Charlie was blamed.

In March 1995 came the huge shock and terrible news that Ronnie Kray had died. This, of course, brought Reggie and Charlie closer together and the photos of the two brothers at Ron's graveside united in grief are still very moving.

Charlie Kray was born for parties and anyone who was lucky enough to party with him will testify to this. He was funny, charming, warm and made everyone welcome, a real people person who bowled people over.

Unfortunately, his warm openness was taken advantage of in one of the biggest, disgusting, most blatant police fit-ups in history. In 1997, Charlie Kray was charged with organising a £39 million cocaine deal. Undercover police, who suspected him, befriended him and hassled him to get drugs for them for about nine months. Eventually, he put them on to someone who may have been able to help them. No drugs were found on him or anywhere near him; no drugs were forthcoming at all. £39 million worth of coke ... it's fucking ridiculous! Charlie was skint most of the time!

That didn't stop them, though, and, in his seventies,

Charlie Kray received 12 years in prison. Unfortunately, around this time, he also lost his son Gary to cancer.

Charles Kray died on 4 April 2000 of complications due to heart trouble in the arms of his closest friend Wilf Pine.

Reading this, you may be thinking, He must have done something really bad to get all that time in prison.

Trust me when I tell you he didn't do anything bad. But he had to be put away ... because his name was Kray.

Ron and Reg Kray

Over 30 books have been written on the Kray twins – some good, some bad. To be honest, so much has been written about them it would be a complete waste of time to go over the same stories for the sake of filling pages. One thing I will say, though, Reg Kray should never have served the amount of time he did. He received a 30-year recommendation in 1968 for the murder of Jack 'The Hat' McVitie. He served 32 years and was only released because the Home Secretary knew he was dying of cancer. It was a cop-out by the Home Office and was typical of their cowardice to make bold decisions. Reg and Ron had become famous and it would have taken a brave Home Secretary to release Reg. Unfortunately, brave politicians who actually listen to the people are extremely rare.

Ron, of course, was a totally different case. He was a sick man and knew Broadmoor Hospital for the Criminally Insane would be his permanent home. Ron died of a heart-attack in March 1995. The 'Colonel' was given a stunning send-off with Dave Courtney overseeing security.

But Reg should have been released; if not before Ron's

The graves of Ronnie and Reggie Kray, with Charlie lying beside them.

death, then certainly after. There would be no argument or room for complaint if every killer received 30 years for murder without exception ... but they don't.

It's because there have been many killers, many of them serial killers responsible for far worse crimes and receiving far shorter sentences, that the amount of time that Reg Kray served for the murder of another gangster who knew the rules is so obviously wrong.

It's these inconsistencies that throw scorn on the lawmakers and their servants.

As I say, if everyone who is convicted of murder draws 30 years (or serves 32 in Reg's case) then, at worst, it could be seen as hard but fair. But, when endless scum who abuse children are constantly receiving far softer punishment, you really have to worry.

Maybe the twins did not really get so long because of two gangland murders. Maybe they got 30 years because they embarrassed Lords like Boothby. In short, they may have known too much.

For those who don't know the full story of the Kray twins, I recommend the following books. For the gangster years, you still can't beat the classic *A Profession of Violence* by John Pearson. Pearson's follow-up, *The Cult of Violence*, is also a must-read.

For the twins' prison and final years, I recommend *The Krays and Me* by Charlie Bronson.

If you really want to get into the Kray story, you certainly won't find books on them hard to find. Something tells me, though, there will be a lot more books on them to come.

The 'Warriers IV' show held in honour of Charlie Bronson.

Chris Lambrianou

What a great fella Chris is. He and Tony were like chalk and cheese; two totally different people could not be found. Chris and Tony had many a fall-out, but the bond was always there.

Chris and Tony Lambrianou were both sentenced to 15 years for their part in the disposal of the body of Jack 'The Hat' McVitie in October 1967. There is little doubt they were dropped right in the shit. After Reggie Kray had stabbed Jack, he turned to Tony and said, 'Get rid of that,' and, with that, the twins were gone.

They rolled Jack up and put him across the back seat of his beaten-up old Ford Zodiac, complete with broken headlights and no windscreen wipers. Tony drove the car down the Rotherhithe Tunnel while Chris followed. The car was running out of petrol and came chugging to a halt outside a church ... right on Freddie Foreman's manor!
When Ronnie Kray found out where the car was left, he went hysterical. Once again, Freddie was left to clear up the aftermath of a Kray night out.

Chris Lambrianou had taken no part in the murder; he actually liked Jack. I don't think Chris had any idea what was planned for Jack that night. As far as he knew, himself, Tony and the Mills brothers, Ray and Allan, were just going to a Saturday-night party. Now they were accessories to murder.

After the sentences were dished out, Chris did not settle down and do his time like a good boy. He fought all the way and had plenty of run-ins with screws and cons alike. Chris is one of the only men to have landed one on Ian Brady. A knighthood is surely in order for that.

It was while in prison that Chris became a Christian. Chris is not one of those who push religion on you. He will talk about it if you ask him but he's certainly no Bible basher. He is an interesting and intelligent man. Chris has helped many young people beat addiction at the Ley Community in Oxford. A thorough account of his life can be found in his book *Escape from the Kray Madness*. The good Chris has done far outweighs the bad.

We must also mention Jimmy Lambrianou, who is another great guy.

Chris Lambrianou is living proof of how much people can change if they really want to. Good on you, Chris.

Tony Lambrianou

On 26 February 2004, Tel Currie decided to dedicate the 'Warriors IV' unlicensed fight show to Charlie Bronson. Charlie's appeal was coming up on 1 April, and Tel wanted to raise some awareness for it. It struck him (and still does today) that, when you mentioned the name Charlie Bronson to the public, they would say things like 'lunatic', 'madman' and even 'killer'. When questioned further as to how they had reached these drastic conclusions, they didn't have a clue.

'Oh, I thought he had killed people ... oh well.'

The bold aim of 'Warriors IV' was to put a few facts across.

Tel remembers, 'On the way to the venue, my phone rang and it was Roy Shaw. I nearly crashed the car when he told me, "Telboy, I just heard. Tony Lambrianou died yesterday."

'I rang and told Ricky English who was already at the venue. I am told he just about saved himself from falling down with shock. At the venue, I numbly started putting the

Tony Lambrianou and Tel Currie.

name cards on the VIP tables. Roy Shaw, Joey Pyle, Johnny Frankham, Alfie Hutchinson ... It wasn't until I got to the one that said "Reserved for Tony Lambrianou" that it finally hit home. I still have that sign. I had only spoken to Tony two days before to check he was still coming to the show. He responded in his usual chirpy way, "I won't let you down, Tel. Will Roy, Joe and Alfie be there? Great stuff. See you there."

'Ricky English, to his eternal credit, hastily started the show with a moving tribute and a minute's silence for Tony. It was the only time I could ever remember Tony missing a fight show.

'There have been many different opinions published about Tony. Charlie Bronson's opinion is covered in his book *The Krays and Me*. My own opinion of the man differs from Charlie's. Like everyone, Tony had his faults but, unlike a lot of people, his good qualities far outweighed them. The fact that I smile when I think of him says it all, really. He lived for his Wendy and he lived for his friends, and he wasn't afraid to admit that he looked up to Joey Pyle, Freddie Foreman and Roy Shaw. He was also great value at the boxing shows. He told everyone what they wanted to hear about the twins, and played the part of the '60s gangster if that's what made people happy; he was a real crowd pleaser.

'Tony Lambrianou was never as high up the pecking order as Freddie Foreman, Charlie Richardson, Joey Pyle or Roy Shaw, but, as far as I knew, he never claimed he was either.'

Tony's funeral on 11 March 2004 was awash with famous faces from all walks of life. The wake held at Charlie Magri's pub in the East End was jam packed. It was a big send-off but still retained its intimacy.

If you want to know more about Tony, it's all in his book, *Inside the Firm*.

Tony, rest in peace, mate.

Carlton Leach

Although originally an East End boy, Carlton is known as one of the original Essex boys. The reign of the notorious Essex firm came to a bloody halt in December 1995 when his pals Pat Tate and Craig Rolfe, along with his best friend Tony Tucker, were blasted to death in a Range Rover near the village of Rettendon in Essex.

Carlton knows he could well have been in that Range Rover that night and a dark side of him wishes he was. The effect Tony's death had on him cannot be described in words and he still feels the pain today. But people like Carlton Leach don't stay down for long; they are winners, survivors and they fight on.

The Range Rover murders aside, Carlton has an amazing story to tell, as can be seen in his book *Muscle*. He started his roller-coaster life of violence scrapping on the football terraces as a passionate West Ham fanatic and loving every minute of it.

As he matured, he worked the toughest doors in a time when doormen had to be real fighters, and Carlton Leach was, and is, a real fighter. His reputation soon carried him to head-doorman status at one of Britain's most sought-after and fought-after doors, The Ministry of Sound. Here, he fought off opposition from Lenny McLean, amongst many others. If you wanted to muscle in on Carlton's doors, you had to be prepared to get hurt ... or worse.

Carlton Leach and the boys.

Carlton's reputation was respected enough for him to be head-hunted by leading underworld figures to mind millions of pounds of cash and he is one of Britain's leading debt collectors; if muscle for hire is what you're after, then Carlton Leach is your man.

He has been shot at, stabbed, glassed and even had an axe in his head, but Carlton considers that par for the course. Carlton was also minder and close friend to former middleweight and super-middleweight world champion Nigel Benn.

Everyone respects Carlton, particularly because of his loyalty to his true friends; he was there at 'Warriors IV' supporting Charlie all the way. Carlton is a true gentleman and, I am sure you will agree, deserves his place in this book as a true legend.

John Lennon

No ... *not* the Beatle! He was the scum who abused old ladies. It was in Risley Jail in 1985 that Charlie bumped into him ... at 40 miles per hour!

Like all low-life rats, he made a statement; but pigs squeal, it's to be expected.

For once, the Old Bill gave Charlie a break; they must have despised him as much as everyone else.

He got lifed off, and let's hope he's still locked up.

Mark Lewis

This scum copped three-and-a-half years for having it off with a young girl and being involved in a threesome. You can trust *nobody* when kids are involved. Judge Giles Forrester branded Lewis 'a perverted and depraved man'.

Let's just call him an evil bastard ... why mince words?

Denny Mancini

Another of Britian's greatest boxing trainers and the best cuts man that ever lived. Denny worked with all the great British champions and was loved and respected by all of them. Great trainers of the Denny Mancini, Jimmy Tibbs and Johnny Bloomfield mould are now getting very thin on the ground and it's a tragedy.

Denny Mancini passed away on 10 September 2004, aged 71. Rest in peace, Denny.

Howard Marks

Howard Marks was, without question, the 'King of the Cannabis Smugglers'.

The Welsh 'Mr Nice' handled up to 50 tons of the stuff in one go and had untold identities. Howard had connections with the Mafia, the IRA, the CIA and God knows who else. He really was 'big time'!

Howard is a charming, funny bloke and is impossible to dislike. There are far too many Howard Marks stories for this book, and he has been written about in depth in many others. The best book of the lot is the man's autobiography called *Mr Nice*.

Howard Marks's empire came crashing down thanks to a grass. One of Howard's 'pals' told everything to the police while he was wired up. Howard served seven years in America and is now back in the UK. He has written books and does a great one-man show throughout the country.

Eric Mason

This man has been there, done it and invented the T-shirt. Eric Mason is one of the most respected underworld faces of the last 50-plus years. He was the very last man to receive the cat-'o-nine-tails and was once described as the most dangerous man in the penal system. Eric had an extremely close relationship with the Kray brothers and supported them unflinchingly right up until their deaths. Eric was what the underworld call 'a pavement artist' – in other words, a robber.

In prison, Eric became a legend. Like all real underworld legends, he was no bully but would not take shit from anyone, cons or screws alike. He got the lot – the cat-'o-nine-tails, the birch, bread and water, straitjackets, countless beatings from mobs of screws, solitary confinement ... you name it.

In 1959, Eric found himself in HMP Wandsworth with a man named Reg Kray; they got on instantly. Eric and Reg used to find out who the nonces were and gave the bastards a good kicking ... good on 'em!

Unlike many people around the Krays, Eric's support and loyalty never faltered and, in return, the brothers had the utmost respect for him as a face in his own right. Eric was also a good businessman and owned the hugely successful Brown Derby club.

Eric is currently back inside for a right liberty of a sentence, but the man himself will explain all about that in his new book. If you want to learn about underworld history and the real truth, you can't go wrong with Eric Mason's books.

Eric Mason is a true gentleman but, like most gentlemen, taking his kindness as weakness would be a huge mistake, as he does not suffer fools gladly. This man deserves real respect. Who else can get an axe in the canister and survive?

I could write pages on Eric but the best thing to do is read the man's own books. Eric, I wish you well and look forward to you telling the world the *real* truth behind your last conviction.

Micky McAvoy

One nice fella, if not the best! He got 25 years for the Brinks Mat gold job. Micky let Charlie have his boxing gloves, and he remembers, 'I treasured them and, believe me, they got some good use! Last time I saw Micky was in Full Sutton Jail in the 1990s. He's out now and doing magic! A top legend, solid and staunch.'

That was a fucking big sentence he survived there. Twenty-five years is no joke. He spent a good ten years of it on the special units. It's not easy on high-risk status, you can't see who you want, you can't have contact with who you want, every day is 'double' security, double checks, you're no longer a human, you're an animal. They de-humanise you, years of pressure, they rule your whole existence, they take over.

It takes a big man to survive such a sentence and Micky McAvoy is the man – respect!

Lenny McLean

Lenny McLean was a doorman when he took up unlicensed boxing. His story has been told many times and it's all in his book *The Guv'nor*. That book has been widely criticised for not including the six losses out of 12 fights Lenny suffered in the ring, but it was a number-one bestseller and is still selling like hot cakes.

Lenny and Roy Shaw are, of course, the first names people will come up with if you ask them to name unlicensed fighters or British hard men, but Lenny had other talents. His parts as Barry the Baptist in the classic film *Lock, Stock and Two Smoking Barrels* and TV's *The Knock* showed his attributes as an actor.

Tragically, Lenny didn't get to see his new career take off. He died of cancer on 28 July 1998.

Jack 'The Hat' McVitie

Anyone who knows anything about the UK underworld will have heard of Jack McVitie. The image you have is most likely of a drug-ravaged, drunk, crazy, big-mouth coward.

That, at least, is how he is portrayed in the film *The Krays*. The Krays, of course, had their reasons for killing McVitie – and this is in no way a criticism of them – but there was more to Jack McVitie than the image described above. In the last couple of years of his life, the description is probably pretty true but let's get it in proportion. Jack 'The Hat' was not a nonce or a grass and he had one thing that all hard men have – bottle!

Respected men like Roy Shaw, Frankie Fraser and Joey Pyle will vouch for the courage Jack had in the early days before the drink and drugs took hold. Roy Shaw, one of the toughest men ever to serve time in a British jail, recalls, 'When we did the nonces, Jack McVitie was always with me, he was as game as a bagel.'

Tony Lambrianou, who witnessed the killing of McVitie in the basement flat in Evering Road, Stoke Newington, London, on 28 October 1967, says, 'All that about him diving through a window to escape was complete rubbish, it never happened. He actually punched the window in temper, took his jacket off and turned to have a row with them muttering, "Who the fuck do they think they are?" and he never said, "I'll be a man but I don't want to die like one ..." Fuck knows where that crap came from!'

Joey Pyle adds, 'Mac got out of order but he didn't deserve to die like that. He died like a rat, like a grass. If he had to go, he deserved better than that. He wasn't scum, he should have gone with some dignity if he had to go at all.'

Of course, you can't go around threatening to shoot the Krays and go causing havoc in Freddie Foreman's casino without coming unstuck. The point is, there were two Jack

'The Hat' McVities. The one who caused havoc and made threats when the pills and booze took hold of his mind, but there was also a brave, hard man with bags of courage who could really have a row. And he also seriously hurt a lot of filthy nonces ... always a plus point, that one!

Richard 'Red' Menzies

It's not only villains and fighters that make legends. Men with hearts of gold also deserve recognition and respect. Richard – or 'Red' to his pals – has for years looked after the great Cliff Fields, unpaid and mostly unthanked. There is no getting away from the fact that Cliffy is suffering very badly from alcoholism and is a very sick man. It is Red who has been there for Cliff every time.

When Cliff entered rehab and consequently fell back off the wagon, Red was there for him, cleaning up. When Cliff was banned from all local pubs and buses, it was Red who was there once again. When Cliff was told Roy Shaw and 'Gypsy' Johnny Frankham were coming to visit him, it was Red who made sure that Cliff had good clean clothes to wear and stayed sober.

Not really an enviable job. Can you imagine trying to stop a 6ft 3in legendary unlicensed boxing champion and former professional fighter, who twice knocked Lenny 'The Guv'nor' McLean spark out, from doing what he wants? And Red is only small!

But Cliff does know he has a hell of a lot to thank his pal Red for and Red has never taken anything from Cliff, just given.

Red, you are a true legend, mate.

Richard 'Red' Menzies

Dennis Mercer

If Charlie was asked who was the maddest fucker he's ever met, this chap would have to come in the top five – some of his stunts just beggar belief.

Dennis was forever in the wars himself; he lived in the next cell to Charlie in Norfolk House in Broadmoor on and off for four years.

He was just one of those nutters you felt compassion for. A truly sad specimen. Charlie witnessed him at his worst; he had it all – injections, electrotherapy, liquid cosh, and lots of kickings, as well as long periods of seclusion.

He would smash his head for hours on the door until blood ran under it, and he once pulled out one of his eyes, so that it dangled on his cheek. He would shit all over his cell, piss through the crack in the door, scream, pull his hair out.

Charlie recalls, 'One day, we were all queueing up for our dinner and he stood in front of us and just shit himself! It was falling out of the bottom of his trousers ... all over the dining-room floor. At other times he would dive on people just for the fun of it. Once I saw him punch a screw and burst out laughing! One day, we were all out on the yard and Dennis began to run round and round fast, like a bat out of hell, but completely naked – with a big hard-on! Then he slips, and has a crap! Then he rubbed the shit all over him and started running again ...

'It was madness at its best ... and it was driving me nuts!'

The Messinas

In the 1930s, the Messina brothers controlled vice in London. Not known as men of many morals, they specialised in brothels and finding the girls to work in them.

Eugenio, Attilio, Carmelo, Salvatore and Alfredo Messina managed to turn the very upmarket Mayfair into the sleaziest area in London.

Their techniques included cutting the fingertips of rival gang members who tried to muscle in on their empire. Some of the girls who worked in their brothels were said to have been subjected to similar or worse treatment.

The brothers were eventually to feature in a *People* newspaper exposé.

They were eventually driven out of England by a mixture of media attention and new, up-and-coming gangsters.

Ray Mills

London's gangland in the 1950s and '60s is mainly associated these days with the East End and South London. This, of course, is a very generalised view, because West London and, in particular, Ladbroke Grove, Notting Hill, Kensal New Town and Paddington were extremely tough and naughty areas. Rumour has it, the Krays came over to West London in a takeover bid ... and were sent straight back to Bethnal Green!

Paddington was, in fact, Jack 'Spot' Comer's manor at one time and was also home to the famous Senior Street Boxing Gym which produced, among others, former World Middleweight Champion Terry Downes. It was also the stomping ground of the worst landlord in history ... Peter Rachman.

In Notting Hill was Rillington Place (no longer there). 10 Rillington Place, of course, was home to one John Christie, one of Britain's worst ever serial killers.

Respected names in this area were Jimmy 'The Paddington

Puncher' Smith, Johnny Hanlon, Dave Barry, Lenny Smithers, Kenny Smith, Charlie Lumley ... and Ray Mills.

Ray Mills's reputation was tried and tested and this was his manor. In the 1950s, Ray became close to another up-and-coming rascal of the time ... Roy Shaw. They remain firm friends to this day. Ray has done his time in Britain's toughest jails alongside the toughest men. He now runs his own successful, legitimate business.

On 28 October 1967, Ray and his brother Allan went for a drink with Chris and Tony Lambrianou. They then went on to the Regency Club, owned by the Kray brothers, and a worse-for-wear Jack 'The Hat' McVitie joined them. As everyone now knows, they then went on to a party in Evering Road, Stoke Newington. The Mills brothers and the Lambrianous were surprised to see Ronnie and Reggie Kray there along with members of their firm. Everyone left the basement flat alive that night ... except Jack.

Neither the Mills brothers nor the Lambrianou brothers knew anything about a set-up; they thought they had bade the twins farewell for the night earlier in the evening at the Carpenter's Arms which belonged to Ron and Reg, so, when Reggie pulled out a gun, aimed it at Jack's head and pulled the trigger, it was a bit of a shock to say the least!

The gun, though, was a 'duff 'un' and failed to fire. A scuffle ensued and all hell broke loose. Ron hit Jack under the eye with a sherry glass and told him to fuck off instead. To everyone's amazement, Jack stood defiantly. According to the lads who were there, the famous story about Jack trying to dive out of the window to escape was 'total bullshit ... he wanted to row with them'.

Jack McVitie was stabbed to death and taken away by Tony Lambrianou. Freddie Foreman was left, yet again to tidy up another twins' night out.

Ray Mills was extremely respected and still is. On 25 February 2004, Tony Lambrianou passed away. He was buried on 11 March with full 'firm' battle honours. At the graveside that freezing day, Roy Shaw, Ray Mills and Alfie Hutchinson stood shoulder to shoulder. As they moved away from the huge floral tributes, Ray embraced and shook hands with another man – Chris Lambrianou. The last time the two men had seen each other was on 28 October 1967 ... in a basement flat in Stoke Newington.

Frank 'The Mad Axeman' Mitchell

Frank Mitchell was killed on Christmas Eve 1966. The Krays had their reasons and this is not criticism but, like McVitie, there were two versions of the same man. Freddie Foreman and Alf Gerrard put an end to the Mitchell story and there is no doubt that, by this time, they had very little choice; but, before this, Mitchell was very popular.

First, Frank was never a 'Mad Axeman' at all and he never killed anyone. In prison, he was an icon to the other inmates. The screws were nothing short of shit scared of him.

He was anti-authority and anti the people who worked for that system. All accounts of Frank Mitchell describe his physical strength as superhuman. He is still known as one of the most powerful men ever in the British penal system. It is also widely accepted that he was a bit backward and not too clever. Some legendary faces, however, dispute this as total rubbish. He was, in fact, very creative when it came to making and repairing things like prisoners' transistor radios.

There is no doubt that Frank would have been free if the twins had not plotted and executed one of the most bizarre and ill-thought-out escapes in underworld history. He was already in an open prison. The twins got him out of prison but put him straight back into another one. It's not like he could go out clubbing, is it? Of course, the plan turned sour and the rest is history.

But Frank Mitchell was more than just a victim. He was, in fact, a prison icon to rank alongside Shaw, Fraser ... and Bronson.

Jimmy Moody

Jimmy Moody started his career as part of Charlie Richardson's so-called 'Torture Gang'. He went on to become known as Britain's most notorious and prolific hit-man. He also took part in some very daring robberies including one where he held up a security van in the middle of the busy Blackwall Tunnel!

His 'Chainsaw Gang' became one of the most successful armed robbery gangs of the 1970s. In 1980, Jimmy escaped from Brixton Prison along with top IRA man Gerald Tuite. While on the run, he became more involved with the IRA and, eventually, he became a hit-man for them. At one stage, he even had the SAS after him.

Jimmy Moody returned to London and was still available for work. Then, Jimmy made a fatal mistake; he killed David Brindle, a member of a very highly respected London family.

On 1 June 1993, James Moody was shot dead in the Royal

Hotel in Hackney, London. The headlines screamed 'DEATH OF A HITMAN'.

Jimmy Moody's career as a hit-man has probably never been equalled but, in the end, did he take one liberty too many?

Alan Mortlock

Alan is a top fight promoter who mainly operates in and around the Essex area putting on first-class unlicensed shows. Alan founded his boxing organisation, the IBA, and has built it up into a formidable stable of talent and great events.

Alan has been a naughty boy in his time and done some real hard living, but he is now a man of God and climbed to the top of his game. You can read about Alan in his book *Meeting the Guv'nor*.

It's not easy to get to the top in the cut-throat world of unlicensed fight promotion ... but Alan Mortlock made it!

Tommy Mulligan

Charlie first met this prat in Parkhurst in the mid-1980s. He killed a teenage girl for his own sadistic pleasure. He came unstuck when he shoved Charlie's mate George Heath, because Charlie chased him to his cell and blacked both his eyes; he looked like a giant panda. Charlie told him, if he so much as looked at George, he would rip his dick off and make him eat it!

The last Charlie heard of Mulligan, he had topped himself in Parkhurst ... Good! One less monster to worry about.

Dennis Nash, 'Birdman of the Asylums'

Forget the Alcatraz Birdman – this chap makes him look like

Peter Pan. Charlie met this loony – who is not related to the London Nashes – in Broadmoor in 1979; to say he was dangerous is the understatement of the year.

After 30+ years caged up, he was still one of the most demented fuckers Charlie had ever met. He had his own bird aviary on Gloucester House, but he never used it just for his budgies. He would slip in there with his boyfriends and kill a few hours pumping away. He was a compulsive gay psycho!

One day, he attacked a rival so violently he almost killed him. At the time, Dennis was in his sixties, so imagine what he had been like in his twenties and thirties!

He was a brilliant card player – if not a genius – at bridge and poker. But even when playing cards his nasty side would slip out.

Charlie recalls, 'It was in 1984 when I left Broadmoor to go to Ashworth Asylum, another max-secure prison cuckoo house ... and who follows me there? Yeah, "The Birdman".

'I was on Hazlett; he was on Gibow, which was next to our exercise yard. One day I was having a jog around in the sunshine and I passed the cell windows on Gibow and I heard a moaning noise.

'The next thing I heard ... "Hi, Charlie ..." It was Dennis with a loony right up his arse pumping away, he was bent over and waving at me as if he was on a balcony eating popcorn.

'I couldn't believe my eyes! In fact, I felt quite sick, I was in shock ... well, it is a nut-house.

'He could also be really annoying and run over, pick up the ball and kick it over the wall and run off laughing!

'Even when we were playing table tennis, he would run up

and grab the ball during a game and run off with it; he was just a fucking idiot. It seemed the more you gave him a clump for it, the more he did it, so we had to put our heads together on this prat ... and came up with an easy solution. We wrapped him up whenever we had a game on and unwrapped him when the game was over – simple! You don't have to be a top professor in psychology to find a solution, just use a bit of logic ... problem solved! No violence needed.

'A couple of years after leaving Ashworth, I was reading a paper in Parkhurst when who should pop up in a big two-page story ... Dennis "Birdman" Nash! He was dressed up like a woman, wanting a sex change!

'By now he's in his seventies, his mind's buggered, he's spent 50 fucking years in the can and then decides to be a woman ... watch out you girls in Holloway! Never mind *Bad Girls*, you're in for a big shock when the Birdman arrives. You just can't make this stuff up!'

Johnny Nash

Known as 'The Peacemaker' throughout the underworld, Johnny Nash and his brothers were right at the top of the pile in the late 1950s and '60s. The Nashes ran and protected clubs throughout the West End with their close friend and ally Joey Pyle Snr. They were a force to be reckoned with and as easily respected as the Krays and Richardsons.

In 1960, Johnny's brother Jimmy Nash, along with Joey Pyle, was arrested for the infamous battle at The Pen Club in the East End where the barman Selwyn Cooney was shot dead and others were seriously injured. Jimmy Nash only just beat the hangman's noose.

Johnny Nash is still held in high esteem and his name commands respect. He is not one for the limelight and doesn't turn up at all the boxing shows, but, if any of his friends ever need him, Johnny Nash is never far away ... a great man and icon.

Frank Newberry, 'The Pervert Pensioner'

It took 30 years for this beast to be nicked. Between 1972 and 1973 he abused a young 13-year-old girl at a riding stable. Like all paedophiles, he thought he could get away with it. Thirty years later, his victim, now in her forties, comes forward. He copped three-and-a-half years at Wood Green Crown Court in London. Not a lot, you may say, but at 66 years of age it's a good kick in the nuts.

Let that be a lesson to all nonces; there is no escape from your warped past.

He lost everything, even his family, the filthy slag. Let's just hope he tops himself like the rat he is. Well done to his victim for having the strength to come forward.

Kenny Noye

Kenny Noye is currently serving life for that infamous 'Road Rage M25 Killing' in 1996. Kenny Noye stabbed Steven Cameron in the ensuing fight. What few people realise – or don't want to realise – is that Steven Cameron, a young, 6ft karate expert, got out first and started laying into Kenny Noye.

Of course, in an ideal world, people would not be stabbed in anger on the roads or anywhere else for that matter. But this is far from an ideal world and things happen in anger, especially if you are attacked. There really has to be a very strong case for self-defence when you go on the facts.

Kenny Noye was also acquitted of the murder of John Fordham ... a policeman.

But, again, look at the facts. John Fordham and his partner were in Kenny's property, in the darkness of night, in full SAS-style balaclavas, night-vision goggles and all-black outfits. Ask yourself – if you had your family indoors and you looked out into your garden and saw two men in the bushes, all in black from head to toe, with balaclavas and night goggles, are you going to think, Oh, it's OK, it's only the police ...? Of course you're not! And would you go out and confront such formidable-looking strangers on your property with nothing in your hands? Of course you fucking wouldn't!

Obviously, a scuffle ensued and John Fordham was stabbed. At no time did Kenny Noye know he was a policeman. They were a secret surveillance team; he wasn't supposed to know they were police. In his mind, they were rapists or crazy murderers coming for him and his family. Any man would have done what Kenny Noye did that night. The jury saw it this way as well, and he was acquitted ... but the police did not forgive or forget this incident and Kenny was a marked man from then on.

So, when the so-called 'M25 Murder' happened and Kenny became a suspect, they must have thought all their Christmases had come at once.

There's no way in the world he was going to walk this time. And, of course, the media made Kenny out to be Charles Manson, Jack the Ripper, Al Capone and Frankenstein all rolled into one.

Ronnie Knight said, 'Of course he's been unlucky. He's had two fights and both died. You can't get any more unlucky than that!'

I think that about sums it up.

Alphi O'Leary

Like his brother Laurie, Alphi O'Leary battled through the debris of the war-battered East End to make himself a better life in the heady world of showbusiness. Alphi was a tough man when he had to be, but more suited the terms 'gentle giant' or 'heart of gold'. Like their friends and fellow East End brothers, Ronnie and Reggie Kray, Laurie and Alphi were extremely close and remained so until Alphi passed away from cancer in 2002.

Alphi came from the poorest part of London to become guitar genius Eric Clapton's trusted right-hand man, travelling the world time and again. He was 100 per cent loyal to Eric and everyone else he considered friends, and Alphi was one of those rare characters everybody loved; he was a very warm man and more than deserves an entry in this book.

To paraphrase some words spoken at Alphi's funeral, 'Alphi is a good, honest, decent, kind and caring human being.'

Rest in peace, mate.

Laurie O'Leary

A lot of people have claimed to be the Krays' lifelong friends and confidants over the years, but only one man can truly and genuinely hold that title ... Laurie O'Leary.

Laurie grew up with the Krays in Bethnal Green, East London, and stayed close to them right up until the three brothers' untimely deaths. Laurie was a pallbearer at both Ronnie and Charlie Kray's funerals.

The notorious Kray brothers are only part of the Laurie O'Leary story; his CV as a tour and club manager is second to none. In 1963, Laurie managed Esmeralda's Barn, which was a club owned by the Krays in Knightsbridge, London. There he booked young and upcoming stars such as Eric Clapton and Mick Fleetwood. In 1966, Laurie was asked to manage Sibylla's with none other than George Harrison. Here, the clientele included The Beatles, The Rolling Stones, Frank Sinatra, Richard Harris and hundreds more legendary names.

In 1968, Laurie managed one of the most legendary nightclubs in swinging London's history – The Speakeasy. Here, The Beatles, The Stones, Led Zeppelin, Jimi Hendrix, Eric Clapton, Cockney Rebel, Bob Marley and Elton John all enjoyed regular visits and jammed at this most famous of venues.

Not one to rest on his laurels, he then became tour manager to Marvin Gaye, Martha and the Vandellas, Edwin Starr, Otis Redding, Chuck Berry, The Chilites, Steve Marriott, Doris Stokes, Barry White and The Drifters.

As you can see, Laurie O'Leary has had a fantastic career and is still going strong. He also one of the nicest men you could wish to meet and has never forgotten his roots.

As far as his good friends, the Krays, are concerned, Laurie saw it all unfold as it happened – the boxing years, the first arrests, national service, the firm, the clubs, the mood swings, the gentlemen, the gang bosses, the prison years, the deaths and the funerals. This is, of course, only an outline of the life and career so far of the living legend that is Laurie O'Leary.

To capture the full, riveting story, read Laurie's book *Ronnie Kray – A Man Among Men*. It's the true story of the Krays by their real lifelong friend and confidant.

Tel adds, 'On April 27th 2005 our great friend Laurie passed away. I have been in regular contact with him for about the last year or so. He was in the middle of writing his own book about the East End of London and sent me extracts ... it was cracking! I hope someone takes what Laurie had written already and gets it out to the public. His physical health was obviously deteriorating but his mind and humour were as sharp as ever. Only a week before Laurie left us, he actually sent me his letters that Ronnie, Reggie and Charlie Kray had sent him over the years with a letter saying. "Tel, I am happy I now know these are in good safe hands." I think this was partly premonition and partly that he was disgusted at the people selling their letters and even taped personal phone calls of Reg and Charlie and selling them for their own profit. I can tell you now, if you ever find me doing that, you have my personal permission to shoot me!

'The saddest thing for myself and Charlie Bronson is that Laurie did not live quite long enough to see this book released. I can tell you in all modesty he was over the moon with this book because his beloved late brother Alphi who worked for Eric Clapton was finally recognised in public and received the credit he deserved. I defy anyone to find anyone who knew Laurie and get a bad word about him ... it won't happen!'

'God bless my friend.'

Tel, Chaz and all your pals.

The Outlaws

The Outlaws are one of the top motorcycle chapters around. I won't name individual names, but all the lads know who they are. They are all held in high regard by 'the chaps' and are present at all the functions, charity nights and boxing shows. They are all very close to Dave Courtney, amongst others.

At Tony Lambrianou's funeral, the Outlaws escorted the procession all the way from Bethnal Green to Southgate Cemetery. It all went smoothly and the cars reached the cemetery in record time. It may not sound a big deal, but it certainly was if you were in that procession with miles of traffic being held up; it was like a military operation.

They really are a great bunch of lads and are bound by their loyalty to one another. Indeed, their values could be considered old school, which is a high compliment these days.

One more thing – all the bad press about bikers terrorising innocent people and causing havoc is bullshit! It certainly is where the Outlaws are concerned, anyway.

Kevin Paddock

Yet another unlicensed legend from the golden era of unlicensed boxing of the 1970s and early '80s when names like Roy 'Pretty Boy' Shaw, Cliff 'Iron Man' Fields, Johnny Waldren and Lenny 'The Guv'nor' McLean ruled supreme. Again, Kevin was a professional boxer before turning unlicensed.

He is the only man to have ever fought both Roy Shaw and Lenny McLean. He beat Lenny on points but lost to 'Pretty Boy' in what was Roy's last unlicensed fight. It says a lot for

Kevin Paddock's courage, chin and defensive boxing skills that he went the full distance with both these men.

Kevin Paddock – like Johnny Waldren and Cliff Fields – might not be a name you're familiar with, but his achievements in the brutal arena of unlicensed boxing speak for themselves.

John 'Goldfinger' Palmer

This man holds the distinction of being Britain's wealthiest criminal. He is reported to be worth hundreds of millions of pounds and is one of the UK's richest men. No wonder he's called 'Goldfinger'!

John Palmer has been linked to the famous Brinks Mat robbery at Heathrow Airport in 1983, although he was found 'not guilty'.

But what made him extremely rich was operating the world's largest time-share fraud. It's rumoured he made in excess of £30 million from his Tenerife timeshare scam alone. He also owns many properties including clubs, hotels and arcades in Tenerife.

Dave Courtney, Seymour Young, Mickey Goldtooth and other members of the Courtney firm managed to find themselves slap bang in the middle of a gang war between John Palmer's boys and Palmer's main rival. They survived … just!

In May 2001, John Palmer copped an eight-year stretch at the Old Bailey. Does crime pay? You decide.

Patel

This monster landed in Parkhurst in the early 1990s. News travels fast in prison and, within an hour of him arriving, the whole jail was on edge. It didn't take long to sort it. Patel was found with a broom stuffed up his arse and a cut throat!

Unfortunately, he survived, but he now has to wear incontinence pants. That will teach the swine for raping little boys, eh?

Ha! We do love a happy ending. One of the lads said, 'I bet he did it to himself ... some folk will do anything for attention.'

Cass Pennant

Cass Pennant is not a gangster or a boxer, but he's had more drama than the entire cast of *EastEnders*!

Violence, out of necessity, became a way of life for this man. His prowess as a street fighter earned him respect and acceptance. Cass has fought with the most vicious thugs and mixed with London's most dangerous villains.

In the late 1970s, one London gang in particular rose to national prominence, West Ham's Inter-City Firm, otherwise known as the ICF. Cass swiftly became one of its most feared generals and fought numerous battles in towns and football grounds throughout the country.

Inevitably, his notoriety made him a real threat to the authorities and, as a consequence, he was sentenced to three years in prison. The severity of the punishment was unprecedented at the time, but served as no deterrent as, a decade on, he returned to prison. Once released, though, Cass turned his attention to making money, with his reputation for violence known and respected throughout London.

The violent world of nightclub security and personal protection offered the best opportunities. Using the organisational skills he learned on the football terraces, he was soon running one of the largest door firms the capital has ever seen.

Cass employed many well-known street fighters and specialised in supplying door teams to the roughest clubs south and east of the river. This strategy was risky, although the rewards were high, until one fateful South London night, Cass's luck finally ran out.

A routine refusal of admission on the door escalated dramatically when a gun was drawn and Cass was shot three times. Close to death, only his immense willpower pulled him through. Cass was then faced with a tough dilemma. The unwritten rule of his lifestyle demanded he seek vengeance. He had a reputation to maintain, but also had a chance to change his life. He took the extremely hard option of not seeking vengeance.

Instead, he began to pursue his life-long dream of becoming a published author. Although the road was hard, his perserverance paid off when his bestselling autobiography, *Cass*, was published. Since then, he has another four books on the shelves.

Cass Pennant has also become an acknowledged authority on the culture of football hooliganism and has acted as an adviser on numerous TV and film projects, including Guy Richie's much acclaimed *Snatch*.

As you can tell, Cass Pennant really is one of the chaps and a well-respected legend.

Good on you, Cass.

Duchy Peter

Duchy is nothing short of amazing! As a child, Duchy was the

Roy Shaw and Cass Pennant.

victim of thalidomide and, as a result, was left with no legs. But he is one of the strongest men there is. He performs press-ups from all sorts of impossible positions, including upside-down, on his crutches, and even up walls!

He is also a martial arts expert and a master on the *nunchakus*. He has also mastered his own unique methods of using his crutches with blistering speed. Duchy is one of the best doormen in the game and loved by all the chaps, not in a patronising way, but because he's bloody good company.

Duchy is also a very talented musician and songwriter. He holds audiences spellbound at the boxing shows by going through his *nunchakus* and press-ups-on-crutches routines, followed by a self-penned song, singing and playing guitar.

The most incredible thing about Duchy is that he makes his disability look like a major advantage. He certainly does things that able-bodied people could only dream of. People don't feel sorry for Duchy or give him sympathetic applause; they admire and respect him and are actually jealous of the bugger!

Duchy's own book will be a spellbinding read. This man is an inspiration to all. Duchy, we salute you!

Wilf Pine

This man is a legend respected by all other legends. He really has seen and done everything. He is well and truly one of 'the chaps'. Charlie and Ronnie Kray counted him as their dearest and most trusted friend and confidant. When Charlie and Reggie Kray passed away, it was Wilf who was by their bedside. Wilf did have his differences with Reg, but Ron said to him, 'Wilf, if anything happens to me, please look after Reg.' As Wilf thought the world of Ronnie, he agreed and, being a man of his word, was with Reggie until the end. Many have claimed to be Kray confidants through the years, but Wilf Pine truly was.

Wilf Pine also has a huge and incredibly rare honour bestowed upon him; he is the only Englishman to be accepted by the leading figures of organised crime in America. He was also trusted enough to be taken to a meeting with Alphonse (funzi) Tierie, the boss of the Genovese family. Wilf, in particular, became extremely close to the very respected Godfather Joe Pagano and the entire Pagano family. Wilf's book *One of the Family: The Englishman and the Mafia* is essential reading.

Wilf even turned his hand to promoting and managed the legendary rockers Black Sabbath, complete with wild front-man Ozzy Osbourne. Not a bad CV by anyone's standards.

Despite all this, family and friends still come first for Wilf and he has suffered more than his share of tragedy. Wilf Pine is, without a doubt, a true legend of the highest order.

Nosher Powell

Nosher has done the lot, a genuine hard man. Professional heavyweight boxer, unlicensed fighter and MC, bare-knuckle warrior, doorman, stuntman and even movie actor!

As an actor and stuntman, Nosher appeared and performed stunts in such classics as *The Italian Job*, *Eat the Rich* and *Superman*.

He was the MC in all the famous unlicensed battles including the Roy Shaw v Lenny McLean classic trilogy. His famous call of 'Bring on the lions ...' has passed into legend.

Freddie Foreman with Wilf Pine.

As a doorman, he took no shit from anyone and even refused entry to the Kray twins when Ronnie and Reggie tried to enter a club Nosher was minding when they were drunk and disorderly.

As a fighter, he sparred with Joe Louis, Sugar Ray Robinson, Muhammad Ali and Roy Shaw. Once on a film set, he knocked the cockiness out of Jean-Claude Van Damme with a single punch!

Now, if that's not a legend ... what is?

Prince Charles

Charlie Bronson says, 'Yeah, I'm not kidding! It was Ashworth Asylum in 1984, which was then called Park Lane Special Hospital.

'Prince Charles came in to open it officially with all the usual red tape bollocks. We all had steaks and ice cream that day!

'On the ward I was on, Hazlett Ward, we were all kept locked in so none of us could get near him. Only special hand-picked lunatics were opened up to meet him.

'Opposite Hazlett Ward was Foster Ward, and we could see the bunch of official prats whisk our Charlie in and out.

'He's only a short arse, and it's true about his ears, they look bigger in the flesh. But old Charlie's not a bad old stick, he gave us all a wave. I think he picked his wave up from Reg Kray.

'Yeah, our Charles in the nut-house for the day, and we all got spoiled rotten!'

Joey Pyle Jnr

Joey Pyle Jnr is, of course, the son of the legendary Joey Pyle Snr. Joey Pyle Snr is a hard act to follow but young Joe has carved out a career, a reputation and respect in his own right.

Joe started boxing about the same time he took his first steps. He had a very promising amateur career, but, like so many potentially good boxers, the temptations of being young were too much and he went off the rails. This combined with a broken leg put paid to a professional career. But, as anyone in the fight game will tell you, boxing never leaves your blood.

Next, Joe turned his hand to promoting and is regarded as one of the best in the country. Joey Pyle Jnr became the youngest ever promoter to stage a title fight when the gypsy fighter Mark Baker beat Ali Forbes at York Hall, Bethnal Green, in 2000. Joe also promoted such talent as Pele Reid and Cornelius Carr.

Joe is now President of the 'Feds Union' which represents and fights for the rights of Britain's many doormen.

One thing is for sure ... there will be much more to come from Joey Pyle Jnr!

Joey Pyle Snr

When it comes to respect, Joey Pyle is at the top of the tree. Joe has been friends with them all ...the Krays, the Richardsons, the Nashes, Freddie Foreman, Roy Shaw, Wilf Pine, Charlie Bronson and even has the respect of the New York 'families'.

Joe started out as a good professional fighter before embarking on his career in organised crime. Joe joined forces with his greatest pals, the Nash family, and forged a formidable team running clubs in the lucrative West End of London.

On 7 February 1960, Joey and his pals walked into The Pen Club in London's East End. By the time they walked out, a man named Selwyn Cooney had been shot dead and others were injured. Typically, to this day, Joey Pyle has refused to name the gunman (if, indeed, he knew who it was). Joe's explanation remains, 'The guy stepped in front of a passing bullet.'

Joe and Jimmy Nash literally and marginally just avoided the hangman's rope much to the displeasure of the authorities. It was plain to all, though, that, from that day, the police had the hump with Joe.

Joe, however, kept going and loved meeting new challenges, including a film production company and management of recording artists. It was Joe who gave us what we now know as unlicensed boxing. Upon the release from prison of Joe's close pal Roy 'Pretty Boy' Shaw, Joe set

The legendary Joey Pyle.

out to get his friend some boxing matches. The British Boxing Board refused, however, to give Roy a boxing licence. So, in true Joey Pyle style, he said, 'Fuck you then, I'll do it myself,' or words to that effect. Unlicensed boxing was born!

So next time you watch an unlicensed boxing match, either live or on video, remember Joey Pyle Snr and Roy 'Pretty Boy' Shaw invented it!

Not only that, but against all the odds and despite the efforts of the British Boxing Board to ban it, the sport had become huge, filling out stadiums and even circus tents and gave birth to legends like Lenny McLean, Cliff Fields, Harry Starbuck and, of course, Roy 'Pretty Boy' Shaw. Unlicensed boxing is still thriving today under promoters like Ricky English, Joey Pyle Jnr and Tel Currie, and they owe it all to 'The Man'.

Joe met other challenges and projects head on and, in 1985, was Ronnie Kray's Best Man at his first wedding in Broadmoor. Then, in 1992, the police took their revenge on Joe and charged him with 'Intention to Supply' drugs. Remember, the charge was *'Intention* to supply' not 'supplying'. It all seemed very odd.

Obviously, Joe never complained and did his time like the man he is and was released in 1997. Since then, Joe has concentrated on the music business and married Julie in 2002. He also turns up to support the unlicensed boxing shows he started in the 1970s.

It's hard to speak highly enough of Joey Pyle without sounding over the top, but anyone who knows Joe will agree that, where this man is concerned, no praise is too high.

Mitch Pyle

As you may have guessed, Mitch is a member of that most respected of families, the Pyle family. Mitch is another of those men who are the nicest people you would ever have the pleasure of meeting. But, as with many gentlemen, it would be foolish to take his kindness as weakness.

Mitch is the stepson of the legendary Joey Pyle Snr and can usually be found at Joe's side making sure things go smoothly. If you go to the boxing shows of Joey Pyle Jnr, Ricky English or Tel Currie, you can guarantee Joe and Mitch will be there ... in the VIP seats, of course.

Mitch is also one of London's most highly regarded doorman and in his 16 years on the doors he has looked after every major club in the West End and has seen and been in the middle of more than his fair share of action. Among those who have played a big part in Mitch's life are Darren French, Michael M, Paul Wilson, Kevin Byfield, Warren and Mark, aka 'Trigger'... Good on ya', lads!

Mitch Pyle is what is commonly known in London as a 'diamond' ... long may he sparkle.

Peter Rachman

Ever thought you have a terrible landlord? Think again. Rachman operated in the Notting Hill area of West London. Notting Hill some years back was not the trendy area it is today; it was an extremely rough, tough area with some very naughty faces around. Rachman would use his heavies to evict sitting tenants and fill them with immigrants. These immigrants, with nowhere else to go, were shoved into tiny rooms and charged extortionate rents for the pleasure. With this, Rachman created his very own slums.

The word 'Rachmanism' is actually in the English dictionary, a word used now to describe 'people buying up slums to fill with immigrants and charge extortionate rents'.

Rachman became so powerful, his name even popped up in the infamous Profumo Affair in 1963. Rachman actually owned the house were Mandy Rice-Davies and Christine Keeler plied their trade. He also sold Esmeralda's Barn to the Krays. Ronnie Kray demanded protection money off

Rachman and presented him with an offer he couldn't refuse, so Rachman wrote a cheque to Ronnie ... and it bounced!

Of course, ripping off Ronnie Kray was not one of Rachman's smarter moves and he soon found his heavies vanishing or being given a good hiding. The sale of Esmeralda's was supposed to be the peace offering.

Rachman was extremely powerful and had built an empire. Some say he was evil but some say he was a good man because he actually gave blacks a place to live when nobody would accommodate them. Whatever the opinion, the fact is Rachman was a Polish Jew who escaped the Nazi concentration camps, went through hell in a Russian camp, fled to England ... and built his very own empire.

Bobby Ramsey

When looking at the Kray story, it's obvious the original firm from the billiard-hall days and before was totally different to the firm of the later years. It is commonly accepted that the original firm consisted of men of a higher calibre. One of these men was Bobby Ramsey.

Bobby was an ex-pro boxer but was known more for his booth-fighting and street-fighting skills. Before the Krays, Bobby had also worked for the legendary 'Boss of London's Underworld' Billy Hill and then Jack 'Spot', the other London boss.

Bobby also received seven years for his part in the attack on Terry Martin with Ronnie Kray.

Bobby went on to look after many pubs and clubs and even had small parts in the movies. I'm saddened to say, Bobby Ramsey passed away in 2004. Rest in peace, Bob.

Alan Rayment

Charlie reckons, of all the legends, icons and lunatics in this encyclopaedia of who's who in the good, bad, mad and ugly stakes, he is personally nominating Alan as his number-one man of bottle.

Charlie states, 'He's got more bottle than most tough nuts I've met in my life and I've met them all. Alan's an inspiration to all the invalids on the planet. My pal "Big Tony" Simpson has pushed Alan on to achieve all he has done, even the London Marathon.

'You can't but respect and salute Alan. I take my hat off to you, and I know Big T is double proud of you, as we all are!'

Chris Reed

This man went through sheer hell. Chris spent a total of 20 years in Britain's most notorious asylums, Broadmoor and Ashworth. Happily, Chris is now out and rebuilding his life. It's safe to say that Chris Reed is one of Charlie Bronson's dearest and most trusted friends. On 1 April 2004, Chris turned up to support Charlie at his appeal hearing at the Old Bailey along with Tel Currie, Joey Pyle, Charlie Breaker, Mitch Pyle, Harry Marsden and Di Browne.

There is no form of hell on earth Chris has not seen over the years and the man really does deserve to spend the rest of his days in happiness.

Bruce Reynolds

Bruce Reynolds was the mastermind behind Britain's most notorious modern-day heist – the Great Train Robbery. An

Top: Alan Rayment preparing to go the distance for the London Marathon with 'Big Tony' Simpson.

Above: Proud medal bearers.

estimated £2.5 million was earned on that one job ... and that was in 1963!

Bruce's troops on the job included Charlie Wilson, Ronnie Biggs, 'Buster' Edwards, Roy James and Tommy Wisbey. Eventually, the whole gang bar three members were arrested. It has long been suggested that the gang was the victim of a grass.

Tel Currie with Bruce Reynolds.

The sentences the robbers received were more shocking than the crime itself. Thirty years!

Thirty years for an unarmed robbery; imagine that today. Ronnie Biggs and Charlie Wilson escaped from prison and Bruce was the last to be arrested after five years on the run. An account of Bruce and 'Buster' Edwards's time on the run is shown in the film *Buster*.

Bruce today is a renowned author and always welcome on chaps' nights out. The Great Train Robbery is now a part of folklore and Bruce Reynolds, The Prince of Thieves, was the main man behind it.

Nick Reynolds

Nick, of course, is the son of the genius behind the Great Train Robbery, Bruce Reynolds. Nick spent his early years on the run with Bruce in Mexico and North America after the robbery in 1963. Nick is a flamboyant character and a very talented sculptor with his own studio. Nick's incredible exhibition, *Cons to Icons*, displayed busts of all the chaps, including Bruce Reynolds, Freddie Foreman, Peter Scott, George 'Taters' Chatham, Howard Marks, Ronnie Biggs, Roy Shaw, 'Mad' Frankie Fraser and Dave Courtney. The chaps were so pleased with the sculptures they are now on display in their homes.

Steve 'Columbo' Richards

'Columbo' is a true icon from the unlicensed scene of the 1970s. Columbo trained at the world-famous Thomas a Beckett gym in the Old Kent Road with Roy Shaw and Lenny McLean. 'Columbo' challenged Lenny to a prize fight but the offer was declined. 'Columbo' was the most sparkling character on the scene and unlicensed boxing's greatest-ever showman. He took on the Ali style of clowning, including pretending to be on the verge of being knocked out when hit. But, like Ali, Columbo was always the one doing the knocking out.

Charlie Richardson

Charlie is another of the élite. The respect this man still commands is second to none.

Again, Charlie is a man of pride, loyalty, respect, amazing mental strength and a great businessman. Charlie Richardson is another of the rare few for whom no praise is too high.

Charlie and his younger brother Eddie were dubbed 'The Torture Gang' by the media in the 1960s. Their rivalry with the Kray twins across the river is legendary. There is no doubt only an idiot would try and rip Charlie off for money but there were a surprising lot of idiots about!

In fact, the only people who got hurt by the media-dubbed 'Richardson Gang' were people who owed a lot of money and had no intention of paying it back. Also, all of these alleged victims were well-known criminals and conmen. The gang was alleged to have used a black 'Torture Box' on its victims that sent electric currents through their bodies. This box didn't actually exist!

The only 'box' shown in court was one the prosecution brought along and declared, 'The box used by the Richardson Gang was a bit like this one ...' No 'Torture Box' was ever found in Charlie Richardson's scrap yard or anywhere else, for that matter. The fake 'Torture Box' actually ended up in the museum at Scotland Yard!

Charlie Richardson with Tel Currie.

And all the proven conmen and fraudsters pointing the finger at Charlie, Eddie, Frankie Fraser, Roy Hall, Jimmy Moody and others struggled to get their stories to match. The 'Torture Trial' was a miscarriage of justice. Charlie Richardson was given 25 years! How the fuck do you get 25 years for ABH? How many nonces and killers of innocent people get less than that?

Today, it is accepted that the trial would have been thrown out of court. Still, Charlie served 19 years of the sentence, mostly in high-security prisons, without complaint. Could it be that the rivalry between the Krays and the Richardsons was hyped up and made worse by the media so the police would look like the saviours of the public when they were arrested? The worse the firms were made out to be, the better the authorities would look.

Of course, none of the 'chaps' are angels but that doesn't mean they are guilty of absolutely everything that's aimed at them and 25 years for ABH is an outrage. That charge would never have stood up in a court of law today. That's not a biased view; even barristers will tell you that is the case.

Still, Charlie Richardson is a born winner and today owns his own gold mine in South Africa. The film about his life – *Charlie* – is now out and gives an account of the so-called 'Torture Trial' plus his business in South Africa. Luke Goss turns in a stunning performance as Charlie. Charlie Richardson is a one-off, just ask the chaps. There have been some outrageous liberties taken with Charlie and many lies aimed at him, mostly by proven liars but, whether the authorities like it or not, Charlie Richardson was, and still is ... an icon.

Barry Rondeall

What a nice guy he was. Full of life, fit and strong. He copped a life sentence over a stabbing at a football match. He was only 19 years old at the time.

Charlie recalls, 'One day, he was just doing his time like he always did – gym, running, cooking a meal, the Barry we all knew and loved as a brother. The next, he's carried out a stiff in a zip-up bag. He cut his throat and wrists and bled to death. Nobody knows why, not even a note left! He was only in his early thirties and he had everything to live for, a great family, plenty of good pals.

'Hard men cried that day; believe me, it was so tragic I still think about that day and it really hurts to wonder why.'

Joe Ryan, 'The Everton Nut'

Charlie met Joe in Broadmoor in '79. When it comes to football fanatics, nobody touches Joe, he was Everton mad, blue through and through, he lived and slept Everton.

At times, he ended up in big trouble over it. The rows he got into over football were nobody's business. You only had to mention Everton getting beaten and he was on your back, particularly when they got beaten by Liverpool, he would become a maniac and highly supercharged.

Charlie says he'll never forget one summer day when all hell exploded. Joe lost the plot and attacked a couple of screws. Why? Fuck knows why, probably least of all Joe. So he got injected and was put in an isolation cell next to Charlie, who recalls that 'it started as soon as the injection wore off – BANG ... BANG ... BANG! His door reverberated in my head for hours, he just never fucking stopped, the whole asylum had a headache!

'At 5.00pm, the football scores came in and Everton had got beaten. But I got a screw to go to Joe's door and tell him Everton had won 3–0 and that Alan Ball had got a hat-trick!

'It worked 'cos all the banging stopped and he just sang away 'til he fell asleep. That's how I deal with madmen – make them happy!'

Joe must now be in his seventies or even his eighties, but all you Everton supporters out there can be very proud of Joe Ryan, 'cos through all his mad, bad and ugly years he kept loyal to you lot. Even behind the asylum walls, men of honour stand solid.

Good old Joe – up the Blues!

Darby Sabini

Darby Sabini was the head of the much-respected Sabini family from 'Little Italy' in Clerkenwell, London.

Darby is widely recognised as Britain's first 'Godfather'. He was the first 'King of the Racetracks' and controlled most of the trackside betting. The Sabini headquarters, The Griffin Pub in Clerkenwell, still stands today. The Sabinis were deported from England during the Second World War, and other gangs stepped in but, until then, they were the Guv'nors!

Darby Sabini was even the inspiration for Richard Attenborough's character 'Pinkie' in the classic film *Brighton Rock*.

Scotland Yard Commander John Capstick said, 'Compared to Darby Sabini, all the other British gang leaders down the ages have been merely messenger boys.'

Says it all ...

Freddie Sansom

Every well-respected face I have ever spoken to holds Freddie Sansom in the highest regard. In many ways, Freddie is one of those who is rarely mentioned but definitely should be. Eric Mason, Roy Shaw, Charlie Richardson, Chris Lambrianou and 'Mad' Frankie Fraser are just a few legends who have maximum respect for and fondest memories of Freddie.

Freddie was the uncle of the former England, Arsenal and Crystal Palace football star Kenny Sansom. He was also one of the gamest, staunchest and toughest men in the British penal system. He was a great ally to the cons but a nightmare to the screws and governors. Freddie was convicted for a robbery with another prison hard man called Mark Owens.

Tragically, Freddie died in Hull Prison from what was thought to be an epileptic fit. Freddie's death greatly affected everyone who knew him and his friends have never completely got over it. Chris Lambrianou took Freddie's death extremely hard. Chris was the main one to encourage us to put Fred in this book ... thanks, Chris.

So, we salute the life and memory of Freddie Sansom. A great man and friend to all who knew him.

RIP, Fred.

Saunders, 'The Werewolf'

Charlie moved out of Broadmoor just before this child rapist arrived in the mid-1980s. He still remembers 'The Werewolf'.

He later went to Ashworth Asylum which is more secure than Broadmoor. Ten years later, he's still there ... let's hope he's either dead or still there in 30.

A good pal of Charlie's in Ashworth had words with 'The Werewolf'. Like all nonces, he became a whimpering wreck – 'Please don't hit me,' he cried. This bloke put young, helpless kids through hell and he's crying about getting hurt!

That just about sums him and all nonces up.

Peter Scott

Legendary cat burglar Peter Scott learned his trade from the likes of George 'Taters' Chatham and modelled himself on Raffles. Peter became known as 'The Human Fly' and 'The Gentleman Thief'. His most famous haul was the theft of

Sophia Loren's jewels who, in turn, put a gypsy curse on him. Peter's target was always the rich and famous and his career tally is estimated at between £30 and £50 million. The classic 1968 film *He Who Rides a Tiger* was based on the exploits of Peter Scott.

In 1998, he was sent back to jail for his part in the theft of a Picasso painting. His book *Gentleman Thief* is a classic.

Gary Shaw

It can't be easy being the son of a living legend, especially when you're the son of Roy 'Pretty Boy' Shaw and especially if you decide to take up unlicensed fighting! But Gary Shaw has forged his own reputation as one of the best-unlicensed fighters on the circuit. Gary is known for his durability and heart. He also possesses a quality that is all but dead, even in the professional ring ... he is willing to fight anyone!

If you watch Gary in action, you will see what I mean about his durability. This man is a true warrior ... I doubt we have heard the last from Gary Shaw.

Roy 'Pretty Boy' Shaw

The title 'hard man' was invented for Roy Shaw. Some can have a row, but Roy is in a totally different league. Even if you ask hard men to name a hard man, chances are they will name Roy. Roy was a legend in the underworld long before his good friend Joey Pyle literally saved him from dying in Broadmoor's notorious dungeons and set Roy up in one of the first ever unlicensed fights.

Roy was initially a professional middleweight boxer winning ten fights out of ten with six knockouts, but the pickings were better in the armed robbery game. In 1963, Roy was sentenced to 18 years' imprisonment for what was a record-breaking armed robbery on a security van. The judges must have thought that was the end of him ... but they were so wrong!

Roy exploded in prison. Attacks on prison officers and fights with other cons with reputations were everyday occurrences and the system simply could not handle him. He saw the screws as the enemy and he was at war.

The screws would tussle with Roy with batons and shields over and over again, but it just made him angrier and more determined to win his war. On two legendary occasions, Roy actually broke his cell door down from the inside. Think about that for a second. He also loved seriously hurting nonces (sex cases) ... instant knighthood for anyone who does that, I think.

Roy was out of control and uncontrollable, he was

Gary Shaw

simply too violent for the system. Only one place was left – Broadmoor Hospital for the criminally insane, where the 'liquid cosh' was waiting for him. Although now looking through a constant drug haze, Roy carried on his war with the system. Even when barely able to stand through the drugs they injected into him, he continued to throw punches and headbutt any screw he could get his hands on. It really is something when you are considered too violent for Broadmoor!

Roy was now being kept in Broadmoor's hellholes or dungeons. He was in solitary, in total darkness, drugged up and being treated with electric shocks and injections; they even tried inserting needles into his brain.

He had learned to live like a wild animal in a cage and, on the rare occasions his cell door opened, he instinctively charged for the door to damage whoever was there.
This was hell, the bowels of the earth ... but Roy was still fighting them.

Something had to give; if he carried on like this, Roy would be dead in months, probably weeks.

The turning point came when his old pal Joey Pyle visited him and told him straight the trouble he was in, and that he would die in Broadmoor if he carried on his one-man war with the system. Fortunately, as people tend to do when Joe speaks, Roy listened.

He was now on a different mission ... to win his freedom. He settled down as best he could and was eventually released. Now Roy faced a different problem – earning money.

So Roy 'Pretty Boy' Shaw became Britain's first unlicensed fighter and remains, to this day, its most famous and legendary name. It all started with 'a fight to the death' against well-known hard man, ex-con and bare-knuckle fighter Donny 'The Bull' Adams in a packed circus tent near Windsor. Roy's total annihilation of Adams in the first seconds of Round One was one of, if not the most savage and brutal fights ever witnessed and made front-page headlines.

Father and son, Roy and Gary Shaw.

Roy continued to destroy every opponent put in front of him, including Ron 'The Butcher' Stander who had fought for Joe Frazier's world heavyweight crown. Roy stopped Stander in three rounds.

Next up came a man who would also become legendary – Lenny McLean. In a regular ring, this fight would have not been allowed to take place. McLean was 13 years younger, 7in taller and about 5st heavier than Roy. It was a natural middleweight against a natural heavyweight.

Amazingly, Roy stopped Lenny McLean in three rounds. McLean said years later of Roy, 'He was the hardest bastard I have ever known'

More challengers came and were very quickly disposed of,

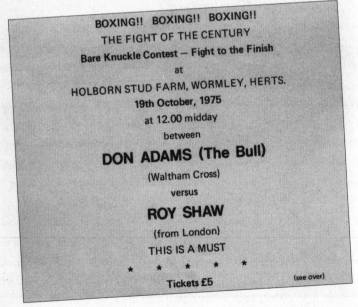

BOXING!! BOXING!! BOXING!!

THE FIGHT OF THE CENTURY

Bare Knuckle Contest — Fight to the Finish

at

HOLBORN STUD FARM, WORMLEY, HERTS.

19th October, 1975

at 12.00 midday

between

DON ADAMS (The Bull)

(Waltham Cross)

versus

ROY SHAW

(from London)

THIS IS A MUST

★ ★ ★ ★ ★

Tickets £5   (see over)

The ticket that started it all off. Donny 'The Bull' Adams versus Roy Shaw.

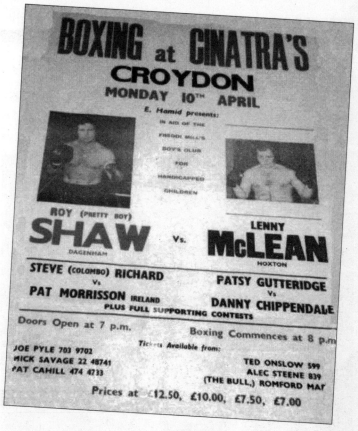

including well-known hard men like Harry 'The Buck' Starbuck and Lou 'Wild Thing' Yates.

Then came two highly controversial and bizarre returns with Lenny McLean. Unbelievably, Roy lost both fights in the first round that caused rumours everything from to Roy betting against himself and throwing the bouts to Roy taking ginseng that sapped his strength and made him 'as weak as a kitten'. Whatever happened, it's still a talking point and many arguments are still had over those fights right up to the present day. Roy's final unlicensed fight was a points win against Kevin Paddock who had previously defeated Lenny McLean.

The money Roy earned in the unlicensed ring he wisely invested in property and he is doing very well today. Roy is the number-one attraction at boxing shows today, but

Roy Shaw – still fighting.

remains understated and unfazed by the 'gangster-celeb' craze.

When you consider Roy was once 'Britain's most dangerous prisoner', and has gone from being beaten with riot sticks and held in the dungeons of Broadmoor, where he was experimented on and given electric shocks with little hope of release, to legitimate millionaire businessman driving a Bentley ... I'm sure you will agree, Roy Shaw is a man to be admired. No less than 35 respected faces have contributed tributes about Roy to his website so far, names that include the Krays, Charlie Richardson, Joey Pyle, Freddie Foreman, Bruce Reynolds, 'Mad' Frankie Fraser, Eric Mason, Charlie Bronson, Stilks, Carlton Leach, 'Gypsy' Johnny Frankham, Jimmy Stockin and Dave Courtney ... Says it all!

Tommy Silverstein

Tommy has been in a max-secure cage in the USA for many years. This guy is inside the belly of the beast. He killed several cons and a guard so his future holds only a black hole, but what a fucking awesome artist the guy is and a very educated fella.

Don't just think this guy is an out-of-control psycho nut; he's far from that. In fact, he could almost be termed a genius. His life was just a road out of madness straight into insanity.

Could it have been the system that drove him nuts? He had never killed outside, only inside. You must ask yourself why? He may not be good, but he's not ugly, and can't really be regarded as mad or bad.

I think he's a product of the brutal system being deployed in the USA. He may have been driven nuts, but his spirit hasn't been broken and it never will be.

Billy 'Teapot' Simpson

Who? Yeah, you may well ask! Old 'Teapot'. Charlie met Billy in Rampton in 1978. Until he met him, he was simply called Billy Simpson. But the day Charlie smashed a teapot over his big, fat, ugly head, a legend was born. Charlie smashed him over an argument at the breakfast table over a spoon of sugar ... well, it was in a fucking asylum.

That's how fucking crazy life can be. From that day to this, Charlie still doesn't know what 'Teapot' was inside for.

Bertie Smalls

Bertie Smalls was actually one of the best armed robbers around in the 1970s. One of the most famous bank robberies of the era, the Wembley job, was the work of Smalls and his gang. On this job, £138,000 was bagged, a lot of money in 1972.

But Bertie Smalls won't be remembered as a good robber. The name Bertie Smalls means only one thing – supergrass. Yes, Smalls was the original scumbag!

The very first supergrass could technically be Albert Donoghue, who was on the Kray firm until things started going wrong, at which point he changed sides; or, indeed, all the criminals who disgustingly put the Richardson firm in the so-called 'Torture Trial' away for so long. But it is Bertie Smalls who still carries the original 'supergrass' title.

What Smalls did is evil. It's about as low as you can get, telling the police everything you know about your friends, shameless in the knowledge that you are taking them away from their families for many years. And all because you have been caught and can't take the punishment that you knew was always a hazard of the occupation you chose to do.

The other thing that grates about supergrasses is that they were usually responsible for more criminal activity than the friends they were putting away.

Bertie Smalls was one of London's most prolific armed robbers; he was no bit player suddenly seeing the error of his ways. Bertie Smalls should have been shot in the head. The fact that he lived saw the supergrass become a phenomenon. If he had been copped for, it would have stopped anyone else becoming a supergrass. Because he lived, Maurice O'Mahoney, Charlie Lowe, Billy Amies, Leroy Davies and many others quickly followed him. O'Mahoney actually called himself 'King Squealer'.

The supergrasses and nonces really are the lowest of the low, the vermin of the world. Hang 'em all high!

Smith

It was in 1999 that Charlie bumped into this evil sod on the high-risk Cat-A unit in Belmarsh Prison. Smith was a giant of a man but a born coward. At this time, Charlie was gradually being let out of solitary to mix with the other high-risk Cat-A cons on the exercise yard. As soon as he clocked Smith, he felt the evil, something about him, he just knew he was iffy. Smith actually told the other cons he was a robber.

When Charlie spoke to him, he had those weird, shifty eyes. Prison is a nest of information and it never takes long to find out who's who; it took two days. He had a history of sex crimes and was on remand for the murder of a prostitute.

After Charlie booted him in the head, he was sent back to solitary. All the lads said Charlie hadn't touched him, but Smith squealed ... and CCTV didn't help. At 6ft 5in and 20st, he was the biggest con Charlie had ever seen. Same old story though, that type are only brave with kids, women and the weak.

The last we heard, he got lifed off and was pumping iron in Whitemoor Jail ... he's probably in training for another round with Charlie!

Billy Smith, 'The Bomb'

Billy is a member of the Smiths/Stockins well-respected travelling family, and is a relative of the Frankhams. Bill's closet friend is his cousin 'Gypsy' Joe Smith, the unbeaten, unlicensed fighter and one of Tel Currie's closest and trusted friends.

Bill really is a formidable cobble/bare-knuckle fighter and has one of the hardest punches Tel's ever witnessed, hence the nickname 'The Bomb'. Fortunately, Billy has never thrown a right-hander at Tel in anger, but he's taken the man on the pads and can safely confirm that Billy's got the most savage punch he's ever felt. Tel says, 'I honestly cannot imagine anyone taking that on the chin and staying conscious.'

But, despite his prowess on the cobbles, Bill, like other fighting members of his family – Joe and Aaron Smith, Jimmy and Wally Stockin, and Johnny and Bobby Frankham – he is a real gentleman and great company ... unless, of course, you are stupid enough to challenge them.

Forget all the clichéd bullshit about gypsies being dirty, rude bullies who leave their rubbish everywhere; it doesn't apply to the Smiths, Stockins, Frankhams or Brazils or any of the other *real* gypsies. They are, in fact, among the proudest, most honourable people there are.

Without getting on our soapbox, the prejudices aimed at the travellers are total nonsense, because they usually come from someone who has never really known one.

Billy Smith would have gone a long way in professional boxing if he had been 100 per cent committed in his teenage years. And he can certainly punch!

Jimmy Smith, 'The Paddington Puncher'

In the 1950s and '60s, Paddington in West London was known for its high output of extremely tough fighting men. World Middleweight Champion Terry Downes was the most famous and the Senior Street Gym is now legendary. But at the top of the Paddington Street fighting pile was the man known as 'The Paddington Puncher' ... Jimmy Smith.

Jimmy was renowned for knocking tough men spark out with a single punch. He usually ended up knocking out three or four men at a time; they rarely came single-handed to find Jimmy. The fights and all-out wars of 'The Paddington Puncher' are still talked about all over London today. Jimmy Smith is a true bare-knuckle, street-fighting warrior of the highest order.

'Gypsy' Joe Smith

This man epitomises the romantic image of the bare-knuckle, unlicensed gypsy warrior, travelling from town to town and beating everybody. Joe was a bare-knuckle king but fancied his chances in the unlicensed ring. He was trained and polished for the ring by Tel Currie and what a dynamic team they became. They both have had amazing experiences along the way, some sad, some extremely funny, but most extremely violent. Joe is currently eight fights undefeated on the unlicensed scene and it seems he is running out of opponents, as nobody will fight him.

He has never looked remotely like losing in any of his fights; in fact, some he carried for a while to get a workout. Joe is rare among unlicensed fighters because he is not just a slugger, he is also a very clever and cagey boxing technician. But, when he wants to mix it, he goes like a whirlwind.

Joe, like his relatives Johnny and Bobby Frankham, and Jimmy and Wally Stockin, is a fighting man of old-school principles. Family first, a hatred of bullies, very polite and courteous, especially around women. These are the real gypsies, not the scumbags that terrorise ordinary folk, bully and leave their rubbish everywhere; the real travellers are pure class and very proud and honourable people; they also despise bullies and will always back the underdog.

So Joe has defeated all before him, on the cobbles and in the ring, but there's a twist to the Joe Smith story. He is also a professional golfer. Don't forget, golf is an upper-class game. It's unusual that a working-class lad can rise through the ranks, but a gypsy fighting boy? That's near enough a miracle. It just shows the heart, courage and unshakable self-belief of this man. Joe's exciting fighting style has made him very popular among gypsies and gorgers (non-gypsies) alike.

'Mad' Teddy Smith

In his final 'confession' screened on TV as *Reggie Kray – The Final Word*, Reg Kray admitted to one other murder. 'Nipper' Read immediately said he thought the victim was 'Mad' Teddy

Smith. Read, who has maintained from the beginning that the Krays killed many more than what is currently believed – Read himself investigated seven murders – is convinced Smith was one of them.

Teddy Smith was a high-ranking member of the firm. Like Ronnie, he was a very dangerous homosexual gangster. Smith was well educated and had written plays and scripts. He appeared in the famous scandal photos with Ronnie Kray, Lord Boothby and Leslie Holt. He was also trusted along with Albert Donoghue to spring Frank 'The Mad Axeman' Mitchell from Dartmoor and looked after him when he was holed up in a flat in Ladysmith Avenue, Barking. It was also Teddy Smith who wrote the famous letter to the newspapers requesting a release date for Mitchell.

But Smith was finding the secrets hard to keep to himself. He was overheard drunk in a pub talking a little too loudly about Frank Mitchell.

One evening, Smith was in a car with Albert Donoghue when he wanted a piss. He popped round the back of the Kray family home in Vallance Road ... and he was never seen again!

When Nipper made his enquiries, he couldn't get any more information than 'Smithy's a gonna!'

A body was never found; he literally vanished off the face of the earth. It's possible that Smith was in deep trouble with the twins, did a runner and got himself a new identity. The twins' driver 'Jack' Frost also disappeared and was assumed killed by the Krays, but he resurfaced again alive and well. Perhaps 'Mad' Teddy Smith will turn up alive and well also ... but don't hold your breath.

'Gypsy' Joe Smith

'Spotty'

Charlie met this screw in Wandsworth in the 1970s. His face was a mass of acne, and it really affected his life so badly that he became the meanest, baddest bastard Charlie had ever met. Honest to God, he was ruthless, kicking cows just for looking at him, even the other screws hated working with him as he was just a miserable git.

He was a big chap, only in his late twenties at the time, but that face made you feel sick. Even his neck was covered in spots, great big spots full of pus and shit. Yuk!

Charlie recalls, 'One day, he was on the servery. I was collecting my soup, and I just poured my bowl of soup over his head! "Good for spots that, boss!" I said.

'I never did last long up on the wings ... I wonder why.'

John Stalker, former Deputy Chief Constable, Greater Manchester Police

This letter was written and sent to Mr Stalker by Charlie Bronson on 20 July 2004 following a pull-out publication in the *News of the World*, listing Charlie Bronson at Number 38 of the 50 most evil criminals – ranking him higher than Roy Whiting, Ian Huntley, Ian Brady, Victor Miller, Rose West, Peter Sutcliffe and just about any other murderer, child molester and killer in Britain.

How a man who has never killed or hurt women and children, an ex-armed robber who never even fired a shot, can be thought of as more evil than these scum is sick in itself!

If anyone can work it out ... please let us know.

Dear Mr Stalker,

I know you're not a silly man, but it amazes me that you can't see the propaganda in helping to keep me inside.

How can I be in the top 50 of Britain's most evil? What have I ever done to deserve such a label? It's just pathetic to even believe it.

I'm writing this to you simply as I feel it's time somebody looked into all this media crap on me.

I am anti-crime and anti-violence, and have been since I married in 2001.

Yes, I bet that surprised you! But it doesn't sell papers when I'm good, does it!

In April 2004, Judge Rose (Lord Justice) admitted at my appeal that I have been brutalised for three decades but now I am a changed man. I cannot express enough just how much I've changed.

You, Mr Stalker, are also a changed man; you're not at all what you once were, what man is? We all grow old, mature and have different views. Just because you are an ex-policeman and I'm an ex-con doesn't make us unchangeable.

When I first got nicked in 1974 – and let me say it was best for everyone that I did get nicked, I deserved all I got – I never cried about my sentence, I saw it as part of my life and I blamed nobody but myself. I was a nasty, dangerous bastard; at 21 years of age I just did not care.

My crimes were bad, but not bad enough to be called 'evil'.

My violence became worse inside, my fight against the system took me to the limit, it drove me mad and I make no bones about it or excuses – I became a very violent man inside prison. The worse I got, the worse the system became with me. It was violence with violence with me, I tore off nine roofs, three times alone in Broadmoor. I'm not proud of it, nor am I ashamed. I've had nine sieges, I've assaulted scores of officers and Governors, so, yes, I've been bad ... but not evil.

It was back in 1981 that I was first labelled a 'mad killer' by the media and not a year has gone by without it cropping up – but I've never stood trial for murder or manslaughter, I've just simply not killed anyone!

I've known of you for years, and I've met cons you have put away. Not once have I heard anyone of them say that they were fitted up, on account you were a fair cop.

You did your homework and got results, you know better than anyone about 'bad cops', but I also know it's the minority. After all, I've had guns in my face! Beatings! Stick-ups! And I still respect the law.

There are also a lot of decent cops doing a good job, so why is it after all your experience of life and hard work as a cop who made it to the top are you letting yourself get mugged off and used?

Do you really believe I fit into the Top 50 Most Evil? Am I really as evil as some of those filth? Child-killers, serial killers, sadistic killers, mad dog killers and rapist predators?

Mr Stalker, please wake up and get a life ...

All it does is hurt my family, disgust my friends and keep me locked up in a solitary cage. Out of my 30 years inside, I have spent 26 years in solitary confinement. I'm still in a cage 23 hours a day, I can't even mix. My visits are closed, I can't even hug my mother. But I am a reformed man!

When I married in 2001, I woke up! I found love! Only

love saved me, Mr Stalker, not prison or psychologists or shit rules. Prison to me is still a hell-hole, full of hypocrites; it doesn't work and it never will.

I woke up! Grew up! And for three-and-a-half years, I'm proud I'm no longer a danger. I actually love life! I love nature! I write poetry, create art and write books, I help many charities. But the media don't want to know the real me, it's the old me they want.

There is now a very serious support campaign to help me get out: www.freebronson.com, and it's the only official site. The other site is not endorsed by me.

I would ask you to try to put it right. If you're half the man I believe you to be, you will at least give it some thought, if it's only in fairness and morals.

When your head hits the pillow at night, ask yourself this – did Bronson deserve to be in that Top 50? If you still believe it, then live with it. I've tried so hard, Mr Stalker, to change, and I'm actually proud of myself in how I am today. I now have responsibilities. I have a beautiful wife and a lovely stepdaughter who loves me; I have a job waiting for me (yes, a job). I have lots of smashing friends; I have a new life outside, just waiting.

But I'll never make it with such a label!

I've lived with the evil scum of the earth, I've seen how they are, how they tick. How the paedophiles stick together. Prison breeds these evil scum; killers are not born, they're created. I escaped my violent life with love; only love can save any man.

I now say one thing – I don't class all coppers as evil, so why are all cons classed evil?

I wish you no harm, Mr Stalker, but please digest it all. If *you don't wish to comment or reply to me, then do it via my solicitor. Also, bear in mind that this Top 50 crap has hurt my elderly mother, it's upset my wife and stepdaughter and it's really told me that I'm still being labelled as something I've left behind me.*

It's really sad and unjustified.

Charlie Bronson
Bronson 1314
HMP Wakefield

P.S. For what it's worth, Mr Stalker, I had 'Bronson' picked for me when I was a prizefighter by my fight manager. My only idol was my dad!

And it's me in a cage 'isolated', whilst the real evil scum are up on their lovely wings playing bingo ... wake up!

Harry 'The Buck' Starbuck

Another of the cream of the great years of unlicensed and another true gentleman. Harry was from South London and had close ties with Eddie Richardson, younger brother of Charlie. He was one of the most respected doormen and looked after many of the roughest pubs and clubs in the toughest areas. Dave Courtney ranks Harry as one of the best doormen he has ever seen.

Harry had a long unbeaten run in the prize ring until he lost to Roy Shaw, a fight he was red-hot favourite to win. At the time of this fight, Harry was widely regarded as The Guv'nor. That's no mean feat when you consider the men who were active in those days.

Jason Statham

Another of the 'Brit Pack' and what a talent!

You will know Jason most famously from *Lock, Stock and Two Smoking Barrels* and *Snatch*. He has also conquered that rarest of British entertainment achievements and cracked America. His role as Monk in *Mean Machine* was breathtaking. And what about Jason Statham playing a very convincing Charlie Bronson?

Greg and Alex Steen

Greg is a well-known London boxing promoter and manager. He has promoted over 100 tournaments in England, Wales and the USA. He has also managed two World Champions, Dennis Andries and Johnny Nelson, and two WBC International Champions, the popular Louis Gent, who boxed Nigel Benn for the world title at London's Olympia, and Nigerian Hunter Clay, who was All-African Champion, as well as holding down the WBC International crown. When Hunter won the latter championship, he had been undefeated for nine years, quite an achievement.

In addition, Greg also managed or had promotional deals with many European, British and other national champions and area champions, including David Pearce, former British Heavyweight Champion; Billy Aird, former leading heavyweight contender; John L Gardener, former British, Commonwealth and European Heavyweight Champion; Ali Forbes, former British Super-Middleweight Champion; Lester Jacobs, undefeated WBF World and European Champion; and Harry Cowap, former All-Irish Light-Heavyweight Champion. Notable area champions include Winston Spencer and Bobby

Frankham. There are many other notable boxers in addtion to these who are too numerous too mention.

As a promoter, Greg has promoted shows in places as diverse as Watford Town Hall, London's Lyceum in the Strand, Leeds Town Hall and Leeds University, The National Sports Centre and, curiously enough, the Cobbo Hall in Detroit, USA, where he co-promoted a world title fight featuring the legendary Thomas 'Hitman' Hearns.

Greg has always had a very much hands-on relationship with his boxers and almost always worked the corners on fight nights. Greg's first BBB of C professional tournament was in April 1981 at the Lyceum Ballroom in the heart of London's theatre district.

It was a star-studded event and featured a European Champion, Colin Powers, boxing the Welsh Champion Gary Pearce. The fabulous Diana Dors was the guest of honour and attended with her husband Alan Lake. Among other stars present were the comedian Russ Abbott and film star Ray Winstone.

It was a fantastic show and launched Greg's promotional career. Since that time, in addition to running shows alone, he also co-promoted with the likes of Barry Hearn, Emmanual Steward, Harry Holland and Joe Pyle. Greg keeps in touch with all the old fighters by being a member of the London Ex-Boxers Association and Greg is also the former Vice-President of the Leeds Ex-Boxers and former President of the Newcastle Ex-Boxers Associations.

In 1997, he was a founder member of the promoters' union known as The Professional Boxing Promoters Association. Over a third of all licensed promoters in the

UK are members and the association has full backing of the British Boxing Board of Control. Greg is the General Secretary of the association and regularly officiates at British Masters Championships.

Recently Greg ran a show with Joe Pyle and some other members of the PBPA at the Equinox nightclub in London's Leicester Square. The venue was packed and everyone had a great night.

Greg and Alex Steen

The late Alex Steen, Greg's dad, was often remembered for his trademark dark glasses. Alex was a highly respected friend and associate of Ronnie and Reggie Kray and also, for many years, the partner of Joe Pyle. The reason he wore the dark glasses was because of a war wound which he received at the battle of Caen shortly after taking part in the D-Day landings.

Alex and Joe Pyle were instrumental in promoting unlicensed boxing featuring Roy Shaw, the original Guv'nor. Roy boxed a succession of tough guys, including former Joe Frazier opponent Ron Stander, and always came out on top until he met up with Lenny McLean.

Alex was also a very successful businessman. In the late 1950s, Alex cornered the market in ticket resales and had almost every tout in London either working directly or indirectly for him. Naturally, there were a couple of challenges to his domination but Alex was fearless and strong and always came out on top.

It wasn't just with touts that Alex made his name. On one occasion, outside the Theatre Royal, Drury Lane, three plain-clothes police officers tried to jump on him and arrest him. Alex, a former undefeated light-heavyweight boxer himself, took on all three officers and battered them all, knocking two of them out cold with the third just lying gasping on the ground. This fight took place in broad daylight in front of many witnesses.

When Alex was subsequently arrested and charged, his solicitor told him to expect a custodial sentence of five to seven years. Alex sacked the solicitor immediately and, though only self-taught, decided to defend himself in court.

Alex read many books on the law before his trial and, fortunately, he was a gifted speaker. In the evidence presented in court, it became apparent that the officers had not identified themselves as police because they stated that Alex knew they were police from previous encounters. This fact, and the fact that they had all taken a beating, meant none of them had taken down any notes. Even though it was clear that all three officers had suffered physical damage, Alex was still found 'not guilty'.

Greg Steen would like to extend his warmest regards and best wishers to Charlie with the sincere hope that the judicial system and powers that be release Charlie straight away.

Les Stevens

Another extremely respected gypsy fighter is Les Stevens from Reading. Les was a first-class professional in the 1970s and fought a classic ten-round war with the Great John Conteh. John was one of the most talented boxers Britain has ever produced, but is unfairly underrated by a nation who seem to dislike winners, especially in sport. Les Stevens gave John Conteh one of the toughest fights of his career.

Les Stevens remains highly respected by gypsies and gorgers (non-gypsies) alike.

Stilks

He has been described as 'Britain's Hardest Bouncer' as well as 'The King of the Doormen' and rightly so. Stellakis Stylianou – or Stilks to his friends – is a remarkable character with an ability to see clearly, act fairly and be prepared to show extreme violence when necessary.

He has risen to the top of the pile by courage, cunning diplomacy and a willingness to go that step further when it's really needed. He is a very loyal friend to have and is one of Charlie Bronson's closest pals. Unless you move in the same circles, you are unlikely to come into contact with this man, but his book *Stilks* will give you a good insight into the amazing life of a one-off.

This man is not just your average doorman; he is a legend, liked, respected and, in certain cases, feared. He is a close and trusted friend of all the chaps and a great guy to party with, but, as is so often the case with the real tough guys, this friendliness can stupidly be mistaken for weakness ... a bad mistake in the case of Mr Stilks!

He is also an expert in judo, winning his black belt by beating a line of six opponents one after the other ... just think about that for a second.

Stilks also commanded security at the funerals of Reg Kray and his close friend Tony Lambrianou.

Stilks is not what you would call 'a tool merchant'; he doesn't need them, his fists and the now legendary 'Stilks Strangle Hold' are more than sufficient to take care of those stupid enough to try and take advantage of this man's kindness. Stilks was the first name Charlie Bronson hand-picked to protect his family at the première of the hit play *Saira*. This was no easy task as there was only Stilks, Tel Currie, Max Icavou, George, Paul and Roley from Norwich in the middle of a hostile 1,000-strong audience. But, as with anything Stilks organises, it all went smoothly, and this was one tasty little team.

Stilks is also a shrewd businessman and has many projects

on the go, including his own nightclub called Faces ... well, what else?

Stilks is also well known and respected for his unswerving loyalty to those he considers his friends and has a strong brothers-in-arms bond with Charlie Bronson. When Chaz is finally released, Stilks will be one of the first names on the party list. I think he could easily fill another two volumes at least with his exploits.

Good on you, Stilks ... you are a true legend!

Tel Currie, Stilks with his brilliant autobiography and Max Ivanou.

Jimmy Stockin

Jimmy and Wally Stockin

By now, everyone who has even a passing interest in bare-knuckle fighting, unlicensed boxing or the gypsy life should have heard of these men. If not, let me mark your card.

Jimmy Stockin is one of the most deadly British bare-knuckle fighters in recent history. A proud gypsy through and through, Jimmy will never and has never conformed to anything or anybody; he is a true gypsy warrior in every sense. Related to the famous Smiths and Frankhams, Jimmy comes from a good fighting pedigree.

Jimmy's brother Wally is also a very good fighter and an extremely respected man. Both Jimmy and Wally suffered tragedy when their father was killed in 1979, but born warriors don't stay down, they come back stronger, and that's exactly what Jimmy and Wally did. Neither Jimmy nor Wally is a physically huge man, but their hearts are massive and filled with a lion's courage. Warriors like these are born, not made. Despite winning many gruelling, bloody and unbelievably violent bare-knuckle fights, Jimmy Stockin also had to overcome being put in prison for doing sweet fuck-all. Again, he overcame and carried on.

Recently, with nothing to win and everything to lose, Jimmy Stockin fought an unlicensed bout to help his cousin Joe Smith pull in the punters in a show Joe was promoting. Jimmy, with short notice and minimum training, stepped into the ring with a seasoned, active, very good unlicensed fighter 20 years younger than himself. The fight was a brutal draw. Jimmy's book was out, his reputation secure, yet he risked it all because he loved the challenge of everyone telling him he couldn't win in a million years. Now that's a real warrior!

Wally also stepped into the unlicensed ring recently and convincingly out-pointed a Russian champion.

We would also like to mention Jimmy and Wally's younger sister Suzie, who passed away in the summer of 2004. Greatly missed, rest in peace.

Terry Stone, aka Terry 'Turbo'

Terry was born in South London on 13 January 1971; his

real name is Terence Pettit. Terry grew up on various rough council estates before going off the rails at age 12 when his parents split up. He ended up in constant trouble at school and, on the advice of his head of year, ended up joining the school rugby team and began a career as an amateur boxer. While boxing, Terry had eight fights with five wins and three losses, one of which was for the Surrey Schoolboys title to Richard Williams who, until

Terry Turbo

recently, was the WBU middleweight champion of the world.

Terry went through various jobs until he discovered his true vocation in life ... running clubs.

He started a leaflet distribution company in 1993 called Turbo Promotions which was closely followed by *The Scene Magazine*, then came the birth of what was to become England's biggest drum 'n' bass night, the legendary One Nation, followed by Rave Nation, and then Garage Nation was born with partner Jason Kaye in 1996. The pair bought Dreamscape and Terry dominated the entire club scene from 1993 to 2003 and won four different awards for Best Club, Best Promoter, Largest Club Night and Best Event, not bad for a boy from South London ... but Terry didn't stop there.

He then started an acting career and has appeared in several TV documentaries, various magazines and the national press. His TV appearances include *My Family* and *EastEnders*, and his feature-film credits include *One Man and His Dog*, released in July 2004, and *Hell to Pay*, released August 2004. Terry's performance of a madman villain in Dave Courtney's *Hell to Pay* is nothing short of stunning and left the audiences breathless. Check that film out and you will agree that Terry is one of our finest actors. Since becoming one of the luvvy brigade, our Tel is now known as Terry Stone, so look out for him under that name.

Terry's other recent adventures include opening his exclusive, cutting-edge bar/restaurant called Marrakesh in the heart of Ascot, Berkshire, and he is currently writing what is sure to be a no-holds-barred book about the club scene Terry knows so well. Terry lives with his fiancée Maxine and their young son Alfie, and he has a ten-year-old daughter from a previous relationship.

Terry's past has been often violent and brutal and he is well known as a man you want with you in a row, but, above that, he is a hugely talented film and TV actor. No doubt, Terry Stone will become a household name. You heard it here first. Good on ya, Tel.

'Fearless' Stu Cheshire

Stu Cheshire is a top pal of Charlie's. If you're ever out clubbing in the Worcestershire area, then you're bound to bump into him on the club doors, all 6ft 4in and 17st of him!

Stu is a natural born survivor. If he doesn't have a mob of hooligans on his back once a week, he thinks he's missing out. When he gets fed up sorting out the drunken thugs, he

'Fearless' Stu Cheshire befriends a tiger.

relaxes with the animals he loves. He trusts wild beasts more than he does people. He's not a bad judge, is he?

Eat your heart out, Tarzan.

Suzy

Charlie only met her once at a table-tennis tournament in Broadmoor, 1980. She was a good-looker and only about 25. Charlie wondered what the hell she could have done to be certified mad and sent to that God-forsaken place.

When she told him, he froze and felt sick ... she'd put her baby in the oven.

Evil? Insane? Who cares! It's a fucking act of sick inhumanity ... Evil bitch!

Judge Temple, Liverpool Crown Court

Judge Temple is one of those people you come across rarely in life, a rare breed of judge – a very fair and understanding man.

It was 1985, and Charlie was in the dock at Liverpool Crown Court; he'd ripped off half a lunatic's face in Ashworth Asylum. He was expecting a good ten years to be added to his sentence, if not a life sentence. But, as violent and nasty as his attack had been, he did have serious reasons to do what he did.

Charlie explains, 'I'm not making it right to use violence ... it's wrong and I got punished for it! But this prat I had attacked got just what he deserved in my book. So I explained my actions to Judge Temple the best way I could, without making it sound as though I was in the right or that I enjoyed it.

'I explained that he had written me a very crazy note, which read: "I want to caress you, and do all sorts of naughty things to you, cover you in cream, etc., etc." The loon had flipped to write that sort of shit to a man like me; it's like waving a red flag to a bull.

'Judge Temple weighed it all up. He knew I had been pushed too far; he studied the note, and he studied me. What else could a man like me be expected to do? Buy the loon a tub of cream?'

Tony Thomas

'Big' Tony was born in the fighting town of Merthyr Tydfil in South Wales. He was brought up in one of the roughest council estates in Britain called the Gurnos Estate. On leaving school, Tony took up rugby. At the late age of 26, he fancied a change and tried his hand at amateur boxing. Within three years, Tony had picked up a win out in Italy in an international and had reached two Welsh boxing finals at super-heavyweight.

'Big' Tony was then offered a job and the doors. Putting his boxing skills to use on some of Britain's roughest doors, his reputation as a fighter started to grow as he looked after clubs throughout Wales.

Then, one summer night not so long ago, Tony was involved in a gang fight involving over 30 men. After battling for more than 20 minutes with a dislocated thumb, Tony was knocked out cold by a gin bottle and was stabbed, glassed and beaten to within an inch of his life. His muscle was hanging out of his arm and he had lost pints of blood. Two other doormen battled to get Tony back into the club and saved his life. He subsequently recovered in hospital.

None of this, however, deterred Tony from his job and, where most men would have quit, he was back on the doors within a month ... still in plaster! The fights and brutal violence came thick and fast, but Tony saw off every challenge. More of 'Big' Tony's legendary exploits can be found in the book *Bouncers* by Terry Currie and Julian Davies.

'Big' Tony Thomas has been stabbed, beaten with baseball bats, had iron bars smashed into his head, has been run over by a car and has been involved in too many bare-knuckle fights to count. Yet, like all *real* respected men, Tony is a total gentleman, quietly spoken, hates bullies, is respectful of others and is a great laugh. But, also like many truly hard men, he doesn't suffer fools gladly and can be a fucking animal.

'Big' Tony Thomas

Tony is currently writing a book on the late Lenny McLean. That's sure to be a winner.

Arthur Thompson, 'Glagow's Godfather'

Arthur Thompson controlled Glasgow and commanded respect from his allies and fear from his enemies. He escaped three attempts on his life; the first was when a bomb was put under his car, but Arthur's mother-in-law was killed in the explosion, while the man himself was seriously hurt. The second was when an unknown gunman shot him in the groin. The third was an attempt to run over him in a car. Arthur survived all three attempts.

Arthur was doing extremely well in all many criminal enterprises, but also went into the legitimate scrap-metal business.

Arthur Thompson Jnr – or 'Fat Boy' – had his father's name but that was about it. He had no brains, style, respect or inhibitions about sticking his father's name up all over the place for his own gain. He also went into the drugs trade and drew an 11-year sentence for dealing.

In 1991, Arthur Jnr was shot dead outside his house. The assassins were said to be Paul Ferris, Joe Hanlon, Robert Glover and another man. Paul Ferris was charged with murder and was acquitted.

On the day of Arthur Jnr's funeral, Hanlon and Glover were found shot dead in a car on the funeral route.

Arthur Thompson Snr died of a heart-attack in 1993 aged 62. Scotland will not see his like again.

The Tibbs Family

The Tibbses were another of the families the police turned their attention to after the conviction of the Kray firm. They, along with the Dixons, were expected to try and fill the huge void left by the twins and their gang. But the Tibbs family violence was based more on personal revenge than taking over empires, although they were in the protection game.

Their most notorious feud started in 1967 when a gang member from another family attacked Georgie 'Bogey' Tibbs. The family in question were very well known and from Stepney, East London. Of course, things like that simply cannot be left alone. As Georgie Tibbs was in his sixties at the time, and the gang member was in his twenties, it was viewed as a liberty. The gang member was paid a visit by Jimmy Tibbs, Johnny Tibbs and Georgie's son, young George. The gang member pulled out a shotgun. However, the gun was taken off him and he was smashed in the head with the rifle butt and suffered gunshot wounds to his legs and stomach.

In revenge for this, Robert Tibbs had his throat cut; fortunately, he survived. Revenge attacks swung backwards and forwards at an amazing rate. There were shootings, stabbings and beatings galore.

But the most serious of these came in 1971, when a bomb was put under Jimmy Tibbs' car. Jimmy's four-year-old son was with him in the car. The bomb exploded but, thankfully and miraculously, they both survived.

Out of the two warring families, the police considered the Tibbs family to be the most powerful and arrested them. James Tibbs Snr copped 15 years and Jimmy Tibbs 10 years.

Jimmy Tibbs, of course, went on to become the most respected professional boxing trainer in Great Britain. Think of Jimmy Tibbs now, and you think of top trainer, not ex-gangster, and rightly so. Jimmy took Nigel Benn to world-title glory to name just one glittering achievement. The fact that Jimmy Tibbs's successes as a boxing trainer warrant a book on their own shows how well this legend has done.

America had Angelo Dundee, Eddie Fuch and George Benton ... we have the great Jimmy Tibbs. Give that man a knighthood!

Rickie Tregaski

This guy should have got a gold medal. He cut Sarah Payne's killer Roy Whiting, but he never got a medal for it; instead, he got six years added to his sentence!

There's something wrong with our British justice – Whiting gets a cut face and Rickie gets six years.

What a fucking disgrace!

Tony Tucker

'The Range Rover Murders' in December 1995 in a remote country lane near Rettendon, Essex, have now passed into underworld legend. This triple murder was one of the biggest hits in British gangland history. The three victims found shot dead in the Range Rover were Tony Tucker, Patrick Tate and Craig Rolfe. All three were known as 'The Firm'. They had been lured to the country lane on a pitch-black, freezing December night by people they trusted on the pretext of a drug delivery they planned to rob. The delivery was a fake; it was bait to get them down that track.

Another key member of the 'Essex Boys' gang – or, simply, 'The Firm' – was our close friend Carlton Leach. Carlton is one of the most highly thought-of men in the underworld and knows he could have easily been in that Range Rover that night. Carlton and Tony Tucker were as close as best friends can be; in many ways, brothers in arms.

Like others in this book, people have a fixed image in their minds of Tony Tucker. They think of a drug-crazed, money-mad psychopath who met a justified end that was always going to happen. But this description is possibly true of only the last two years of Tony's life.

Tony Tucker was, in fact, a man with a big heart, true to his friends and respected throughout Essex. Tony and Carlton were both close to boxing legend Nigel Benn. As well as being friends, they also acted as Nigel's minders, confidants and training partners. They would go away to training camp with Nigel and help him prepare. Part of Nigel's training was running up mountains in Tenerife. Nigel says, 'They were there for me and actually did the running with me. They were good friends and never took a penny off me ... never!'

If you look at footage of Nigel Benn's fights, you can see Tony and Carlton by his side as made his way to and from the ring. It was Tony and Carlton who literally carried Nigel back to his dressing room after the classic but brutal world title fight with Gerrald McClellan.

These events alone show that Tucker was no out-of-control drug monster. Such a man could never have lived under the discipline of training camp, neither would they have been tolerated by Nigel Benn or his team. Also, Carlton Leach doesn't suffer fools gladly and is extremely careful about who he befriends. This may be why Carlton never had much time for either Pat Tate or Craig Rolfe. In return, Pat was not overly keen on Carlton, because he was one of the very few men Tate could not intimidate.

Once again, like many others we have tried to present a balanced view of, Tony was no angel, far from it, but neither was he the monster he was made out to be. He got the blame for a lot of things he never did.

A classic example is the death of Kevin Whitaker. It was first thought that Whitaker was forcibly injected with a cocktail of drugs by Tony Tucker and Pat Tate, who then threw the body in a ditch. In fact, neither Tucker nor Tate knew anything about this killing.

It is also agreed that Pat Tate was bad news for Tony Tucker. Of course, Tony was a grown man and has to take responsibility for his own actions and choices, but Tate did have a tremendous influence over him. Carlton says, 'Tony and I went on holiday together. We got away from the madness of Essex and drugs for a while. It was just like old times with my friend back on form. But, when Pat was released from prison, Tony went into a downhill spiral that was agonising to watch. This time, I couldn't help him. I tried, but Pat had a hold over Tony.'

Craig Rolfe was not in the same league as the other two or Carlton Leach. Carlton says, 'Craig was really just a gofer and a groupie. He would do anything to impress Tony and Pat.'

In the end, Tony and Pat Tate were taking liberties all over the place but, as Carlton says, 'The Tony Tucker in his last months was not the Tony I knew, he was a completely different man. The man I knew was a big-hearted, level-headed man who I would listen to and take advice from. Now, the roles had reversed and I was dishing out advice to Tony. The difference is, he was beyond listening. But the man I will always remember was the best friend I ever had.'

The Tony Tucker Carlton knew should be considered when thinking about the man in future. The life of the man involved a lot more than drugs and the Rettendon murders.

Carlton Leach has a film about his life coming out in the near future. I am extremely honoured to be one of the few who have read the script. This film will show the real Tony Tucker as well as many other revelations that will blow your socks off!

Many people have claimed to know the true story of 'The Firm' and claimed undeserved key roles for themselves. But Carlton Leach is really the only man who was close enough to be the Real McCoy!

Ian Walbey

Charlie met Ian in Woodhill CSC Unit; he came from Rampton Asylum for the attempted murder of a lunatic. Ian first got a life sentence for running about with an axe; fortunately, nobody got killed, but plenty got cut up. He left plenty of stitches, soiled pants and nightmares.

Ian's one of those who gets bouts of depression and out comes the razor and – whoosh – blood all over the place, whether his own or yours, he doesn't care.

One day in Woodhill, he got his razor for a shave and he went to work on his face. He cut himself up so badly they had to rush him to an outside hospital. He came back with over

100 stitches and a patch over his damaged eye. The surgeons saved him.

He was later moved back to Rampton cuckoo house ... no prizes for guessing why!

Johnny Waldren

Johnny is an ex-pro boxer but it was in the unlicensed arena that he really made his name. He was not a huge man, but made up for it with heart and a sledgehammer punch.

Johnny Waldren fought Lenny 'The Guv'nor' McLean in the unlicensed ring twice ... and knocked Lenny spark out in less than one round ... twice!

Enough said.

Wally

Wally runs what has to be the ultimate 'chaps' pub, Reunion Jacques in Twickenham. Everyone loves this place. It's been used for important fundraisers like the Ronnie Biggs night out and the tribute night for Tony Lambrianou. Pictures of all the chaps cover the walls and the atmosphere is fantastic. A few Rat Pack records on the system and off we go!

Bobby Warren

Bobby Warren was a close friend of Albert Dimes, aka 'Italian Albert'. Bobby received seven years' imprisonment for slashing Albert Dimes and Billy Hill's arch rival Jack 'Spot'. According to 'Mad' Frankie Fraser (who was there when 'Spot' was cut up), Bobby was nowhere near the place and accused Jack 'Spot' of framing him along with 'Battles' Rossi.

Make no mistake, Bobby Warren was a top face, and never once broke the code of honour that existed in the good old days.

Curtis 'Cocky' Warren

Curtis Warren is what you can safely call 'Premier League'. Curtis was just another Liverpool kid or 'scally' involved in petty crime. But this man's brain is amazing and, from the streets of Liverpool, he became Britain's biggest ever drug baron!

'Cocky' didn't mess about with street-level dealing; his Liverpool mafia's links led directly to the cartels of Colombia and the Turkish heroin godfathers.

Curtis survived the inevitable gang warfare that comes with the territory and was given the title 'Target Number One' by the police. Well, some of the police. Curtis had many high-ranking police officers working for him, apparently.

Curtis 'Cocky' Warren is now banged up in the maximum-security prison of Vught in Holland. Here, he had a bare-knuckle fight with his Turkish cellmate Gema Guclu. Guclu died of a brain haemorrhage the following day. Cocky claimed self-defence but copped another four years on top of the 12-year sentence he was already serving.

Curtis 'Cocky' Warren is said to be worth in excess of £200 million! The authorities don't hold out much hope of ever finding it.

Louis Welch

Darlington travelling man Louis Welch is widely regarded as one of – if not *the* – top bare-knuckle fighter in Britain.

Louis was a professional boxer but gave it up to make his name on the cobbles and in the unlicensed game. He is built like a tank and anyone who has fought him will tell you he punches like one as well. Many men have been called 'The King of the Gypsies', including 'Gypsy' Johnny Frankham, Mark Ripley, Les Stevens and Henry Wharton. Louis Welch can be added to that list. He is unbeaten on the cobbles and in the professional and unlicensed prize rings and will fight any man. For all this, Louis Welch remains a true gentleman.

White

Charlie can't recall his first name, but it doesn't matter as he wasn't human anyway. He's more reptile than human. He arrived at Rampton Asylum in 1978, two weeks after Charlie was sent there. His trial was on the radio and in all the papers so the monster was expected. He was just what was expected in a beast. He had raped and mutilated a ten-year-old girl.

Charlie says, 'My skin started to itch as soon as he walked in. Days later, I strangled the bastard with a tie. He was clinically dead but they brought him back to life with mouth-to-mouth. Fancy giving that mouth-to-mouth ... the thought makes me puke!'

He cost Charlie a whole year in solitary. Who says monsters are extinct?

It's now 26 years since that incident, and Charlie hopes he is still in Rampton ... but he doubts it. That place is actually famous for letting those types out. Trying to 'cure' a monster is like trying to get a cat to look after a mouse, it just won't happen. Anyone who plays about with kids must get the full punishment ... life should mean life.

Ray Winstone

When you think of British hard-man actors, chances are Ray Winstone will be the first name to spring to mind. His performances in classics such as *Scum*, *Nil by Mouth*, *Love, Honour and Obey* and *Sexy Beast* are now stuff of legend. But Ray is not restricted to one role; evidence of this can be seen in *King Arthur* and TV's *Henry VIII*. Ray has also been earmarked to play Roy Shaw in the film of Roy's life.

Ray is, without doubt, a British film legend.

Georgie and Jimmy Woods

Georgie and Jimmy were two of the most respected men in London. They were top villains and thieves and spent as much as they earned. Georgie received a nasty scar on his cheek after an attack with an open razor. The razor attack was a mistake as the man responsible was smashed in the head with an iron bar and had to have a steel plate put in his canister.

This is actually an example of what *real* villains should be about. There was no running to the police by Georgie when he was attacked, he kept quiet and evened up the score his own way ... 'an eye for an eye'.

Seymour Young

Seymour is one of, if not the, most loyal and trusted of Dave Courtney's friends and has proved himself time and again to be staunch and solid to the last. Seymour has been in some major scrapes and seen a hell of a lot of action and has been publicly described by Dave as 'a very naughty boy'! One of Seymour's most notorious adventures took place on the sun-kissed island of Tenerife.

After attending another successful *An Audience with Dave Courtney* on the island, the lads met up with some of Johnny Palmer's boys in Lineker's Bar, and then went on to Bobby's Bar. An Arab-looking guy approached the group and a huge fight broke out with people being hit with truncheons and bottles, and Johnny Palmer's boys took the worst of it.

The following day, Seymour, Dave, Jennifer (Dave's soon-to-be ex-wife), the babysitter and Jensen have all gone to Bobby's Bar. As they walk in, they are greeted by a mob of Arabs going ballistic in Arabic. With this, Seymour decided to go for one of them, only to be confronted with a gun to his head!

The guy with the gun was shouting, 'Get on the floor, get on the floor ...' and let off a warning shot. At this, Dave has come running over and the guy put the gun in Dave's face screaming, 'I'm going to shoot you!'

As the Arab's dragged Seymour to the back of the club, he could hear them still screaming at Dave and Dave replying, 'No, you're not going to shoot me!'

Meanwhile, Seymour took an almighty kick in the eye that splattered wide open. Strangely, but fortunately, after the kick, the Arabs, including the gunmen, all ran off.

Seymour needed stitches in the injured eye and, as he was being stitched, the nurse said to him, 'There's some very dangerous men outside from the island. They want you and they have your friend.' The 'friend', of course, was Dave Courtney.

Seymour then went outside. The Arabs were about fifteen-handed, and screamed, 'You fucking dog, we are going to kill you.'

Seymour went over to where Dave was being held at gunpoint and was forced to kneel with him. Don't forget, all these guys with the guns were hardened criminals. Then a space cruiser pulled up with blackened windows and it dawned on Seymour that they were going to be taken away and killed. Thankfully, the police arrived and this was the first ever time the lads could remember being genuinely pleased to see the Old Bill!

All was sorted in the end (one way or another) but, as Seymour says, 'A lot of people got hurt on that holiday.'

This is just one adventure of Seymour's. There are of course, plenty more. But that 'holiday' has now gone down in UK gangland folklore.

Luckily, our good pal Seymour is still with us ... just!

Poems by Charlie and Tel
Artwork by Charlie

All Dried Up

A hole in the head
The rain pours in
Soaking wet
Drenched
The brain's a swamp
Alive with snakes
Creepy crawlies
Sucking away
Licking you dry
Parasites
Bloodsuckers
Feeding off your face
Breathing in your space
Suffocating your dreams
Choking your destiny
Power freaks

Taking over your existence
Destroying everything you believe in
All you fought for
A lifetime wiped out
Brain dead
Dehumanised
Beyond approach
Highly dangerous
No more insight
No more laughs
No more smiles
No more sweet smells
No more home cooking
No more walking under the stars
Loveless and empty
All dried up

A dead man breathing
Alive but useless
A living death
A stiff moving
The lights blown out
Skin rots away
Eyes melt
Stench sets in
Maggots grow wings
They fly off laughing
With bits of your face
Your flesh
They're stealing your body

The end of the road
The end of your dream
All dried up

Insanity caught you up
Buried you
Wrapped you up in madness
Even the bed bugs are laughing
Hell creeps in
It takes over
Hell rules
Nightmares of a demented brain
Damaged and broken
A tortured mind
A soul on fire
Ablaze
No tears to put it out
Screaming
All fried up
Sizzled
Burn, you bastard
Up in smoke
Like a rasher of bacon
Can't you see it?
Accept reality
Accept yourself
You're just unacceptable
Born a loser
Born to die
Born to be buried

Born insane
A misfit to society
Face facts
Be true to yourself
Stop kidding yourself
Everybody knows
So do you
Go out screaming
Keep on screaming 'til the devils come
Angels in black cloaks
Bite the dog
Don't let it bite you
Look around
Watch the atrocities
The pain of life
Diabolical liberties
Injustices
It's a fucking disgrace
An insult to your intelligence
Human rights
Don't take the piss
What human rights?
There are no rights
Not for you and me
Not for us
We have long lost our rights
It's all one big fucking lie
A piss take
A dream out of control
Treacherous

Deceitful
Filthy lies
Messed up people
Vindictive bastards
Screaming for revenge
Crawling out of the darkness
Vermin on a mission
Chewing you up
Behind every shadow there is a face
Eyes, teeth and claws
Believe it
Watching and waiting
Maybe you're next to get it
Ripped to shreds

Open up your eyes
Or are you afraid to see?
You blind bastard
Stop running from yourself
Stop running from the truth
Running blind
Running into madness
Afraid
Gutless and spineless
Just another rabbit
Caught up in the light
Caught up in the lies
All dried up

Sucked away into oblivion
No way back
Caught up in the net of life
Trapped
Green as a frog
Silly as a goat
Scared shitless
Ba ba black sheep
Have you any wool?
Insanity drives you nuts
You're a nutter
The original fruitcake
The Humpty Dumpty syndrome
Who pushed him?
Or did he fall?
Who fucking pushed Humpty?
Who did it?
Or was it an accident?
Who gives a fuck?
Do you?
Who cares?
Do you?
So what if he was pushed
Fat useless bastard
One less mouth to feed
All the kings' horses and all the kings' men
Couldn't put Humpty together again.
What a load of bollocks!
They never even tried
Why should they?

I bet they pushed Humpty off the wall
Wicked bastards
Shoved him off the edge
Flying all the way
Crash!
Broken to bits
All smashed up
There is no humanity
We all get shoved off
Sooner or later
A one-way trip
You don't come back
It's a journey
No brakes
Not even a steering wheel
Nothing
No seat-belt either
Not even a smile
No way back
No goodbyes either
One-way ticket
All paid up
Your turn to go
First-class
Little Miss Muffett
Sat on her tuffet
Watching you fall
Jack and Jill went up the hill
Laughing all the way
What fucking hill?

Who's jack?
Who's Jill?
What is all this bollocks?
Who teaches us this shit?
Jill could be a slapper
Jack a drug-dealer
Miss Muffett a shoplifter
Get real
Wake up
Who fucking cares any more?
I don't
Do you?
Who does care?

Once you lose your mind
You lose your way
Once you lose your soul
You lose your identity
You lose everything
There can be no tomorrow
It's just vanished
Disappeared
There was no yesterday
Wake up
Get real
It's all dried up
Face facts
It's for real
In your face
Under your skin

Deep inside
There were no three bears
Goldilocks did not exist
Donald fucking duck
Grow up
Three little pigs
Don't make me laugh
They are in the freezer
Pork chops
With the mushrooms
Can't you understand?
Or are you just silly?
Or don't you want to wake up?
Are you afraid to wake up?
What are you scared of?
The truth?
You're scared to face the truth
You're afraid of the isolation
Truth brings a lot of loneliness
Don't fucking tell me about loneliness
I am the number one solitary man
My world is a concrete coffin
I'll tell you about the truth
Come into my room of doom
Emptiness eats into your brain
It chews you up
Spits you out
It rips your fucking face off
Your heart sinks into a black hole
Bottomless

The Good.

The MAD.

TeL- CURRie

THE BAD.

AND THE UGLY.

CHARLIE - BRONSON

Isolation crumbles your bones
Rips you to bits
Eyes turn to marbles
Tearless
Paranoia creeps in
Mental illness
You become a mentalist
A fucked-up machine
The engine blew up
No longer a part of the planet
You are the man on Mars
A beast of Bedlam
Skinned and dissected
Smell of decay
Four walls
A locked door
Windowless
Skyless
Airless
Soundless
No sweet smells

A black hole of despair
Depressed and forgotten
Welcome to my world
My own planet
A world of silence
Trapped in time
Mad dogs are shot
Mad men are caged

Animal rights
Human rights
Animal or man
Beast or human
You fucking decide
What you are
Who you are
My lips remain sewn up
Now who's the Mickey Mouse?
Donald Duck's in the oven
Princess Diana
Let's discuss a real lady
More truth
Who killed the princess?
Was it an accident?
Don't make me laugh
An accident
Some accident
Fate timed that well
She was blown out like a flame
The candle was in a hurricane
Helpless
So alone
She was a threat to the system
A danger to the Royals
It's obvious why
An embarrassment
A problem
So why blow out the flame?
Shame

Guilt
Truth fucking hurts
Lies hurt more
Open up your mind
Grin and bear it
It's a wicked world
Bite the bullet
Don't dare speak up
Choke on it
Die with the secret
It's too painful to live with
Too much to cope with
Stay in a dream
Float away on a cloud
Peacefully
Die a fucking coward
A butterfly without wings
Crippled for ever
Crawling in the shit of life
Why live as a clown?
Nobody is laughing with you
They are laughing at you
You are the fucking joke

God save the Queen
God save the corgis
Lick the dog's ring
You brown-nosed slug
What about Lady Di?
You have a short memory

Or is it just remembering the nice things?
Forget the bad times
Wipe it out of existence
It don't happen
It was all a dream
A cruel trick
God save the Queen
But who saved the princess?
Who saved the poor souls in war?
Their bodies come back in zip-up bags
Some headless
Armless
Legless
Blown to smithereens
Obliterated
God bless Bedlam
The world's an asylum
Who blessed anybody?
No one blessed me
Fuck all this blessing
It gets your head blown off
Knight me
Die for the Queen
On your knees
Watch that sword, it's sharp
Oops ... sorry, I slipped!
Off with your head
Another mistake
Another cover-up
So sorry, accidents do happen

Burn the evidence
He was a lovely man
I'll drink to that
The crematorium is full of lovely bodies
Ashes
Blowing in the wind
Forever fucking blowing
Killed off for all time
You're next
You prat
Bring back Beverley Allitt
A real Hell's fucked-up Angel
A nurse of the darkness
Myra Hindley's twin sister
Hell on earth
Sickos!

Who shot JR?
Who shot Jesse James?
Who took a shot at me?
Coward
Shoot a man in the face
Not in the back
Be a man, not a mouse
Cowards come from behind
Hyenas
Laughing all the way
Laughing all the way to the furnace
The crematorium awaits
Welcome to hell

Make yourself at home
Enjoy it
We will
Any regrets?
I bet
You can open up now
It's all over
It don't matter no more
Nobody cares
Nobody loved you
Fed you shit
Do you wish you was never born?
Was it all a waste of time?
A failure
A freak of nature
Ugly within
A rotten apple
Your brain was rotten
The core of it all
Or was you just evil?
Born bad
A victim
Victimised
Racially abused
Let me tell you something
You were what you were
It's fate
You got what you deserved and plenty of it
Double helpings
The world is a giant growth

A cancerous growth
Eating us all away
Screaming in agony
No time for sanity
It's incurable
Untreatable
Waiting to erupt
Explode
Like a volcano
No time for peace
It's a painful process
Agonising
Death is imminent
Look in the mirror
Alice in Wonderland
A reflection of hopelessness
The Mad Hatter
It's you
You are looking at the problem
A reflection of madness
It's in the eyes
The eyes are the mirrors of the soul
Say hello
It's you
Can you now see it?
Are you that ignorant?
You are the fucking problem
You were born this way, accept it
You can't fight what you can't see
You can't touch it

You can't feel it
So how can you kill it?
You can't hold on to normality
It slips away
So how can you ever win?
You can't turn back time
You are stuck with it
Time is no more
It ran out
Nothing is for ever
Did you think you were immortal?
You fool
Even myths fade away
Who the fuck are you?
A nobody
Not even a has-been
Dragons dry up
Burn out
Blow away
Even the sun will one day stop burning
What then?
Freeze up
We all die freezing
A giant ice cube
One big fucking ice graveyard
14 billion stiffs together
What a way out

Darkness sucks us away
You know it

You always knew it
It's all part of the plan
The journey
Wars
Death and destruction
Out of control world leaders
'Power freaks'
Ruling the planet
Fucking up everything
Killing us off
Thousands at a time
When they choose to
Pushing and showing force
'We rule'
'Do as you are told'
'Or die'
Pushing and pushing
Actions get a reaction
You fight back in vain
You die in a blaze
There never was any glory
That's only in Hollywood movies
More fucking shit
Heroes with plastic faces
False smiles
And big guns
Bang, bang, you're dead!
Artificial blood
Bring back reality
The good old days

When life was simple
We were all silly
Happy souls
Pass the teapot
China cups
Scones and strawberry jam
Home-made of course
The recipe is secret
A family treasure
So don't ask
Flower people
Hippies from heaven
Free love
Lovers gone mad
Simple and silly
Harmless
Like a butterfly
Floating
Hell's fucked-up angels
Daft bastards
Look how hard I am
My bike is bigger than your bike
My axe is sharper than yours
Mods with scooters
Skinheads with boots
And tattoos
I'm hard
Teddy Boys with cut-throats
Fairies with axes
The good old days

Madness unleashed
Bent cops
Crooked lawyers
Geriatric, dribbling judges
Insane jurors
Media assassinations
Characters destroyed
Lock 'em up ... throw away the key
Birch the dogs
Bread and water
Starve the swines
Bring back the cat-o'-nine-tails
We demand justice
Tony Martin is a chess piece
A political pawn
Move him now
Check-mate!
Fuck him good and proper
Whatever suits the system
This penal system
This penal machine
Judical clap-trap
Infested with vermin
Rats on two legs
What a farce

They hanged Ruth Ellis
A crime of passion
Emotionally wrecked
Duress

We stretched her neck
Snapped her spinal cord
Made her swing
How fucking cruel does it get?
You stinking parasites
You hung a love-torn woman
How evil is evil?
How was it ever done?
In France she would have walked free
A crime of passion
What about Derek Bentley?
Let him have it!
We sure let him have it!
We snapped his neck, too
A rope, a trap-door
A lifeless stiff
A young man wasted
Over what?
Lies
Another State murder
Another innocent soul
Society wake up
Stop being hoodwinked
Stop being fed shit
The Birmingham Six
The Guildford Four
The Cardiff Three
The Maguire Seven
Susan May
Winston Silcott

Eddie Browning
Charlie Bronson
Yeah, me
I'm one of them
A travesty of justice
It goes on and on and on
Lie after lie
Fit-up
Somebody has to go down
It won't ever change
How can it?

What comes first
The chicken or the egg?
You can't stop a bullet
Unless you want to die
You can't grab a shadow
It's all dried up
Like Marilyn Monroe
Abused
Used and degraded
Unloved
What is being loved?
It's a figment of the imagination
A dream, a fantasy
A silver cloud
A rainbow
A space in time
It don't last
How can it?

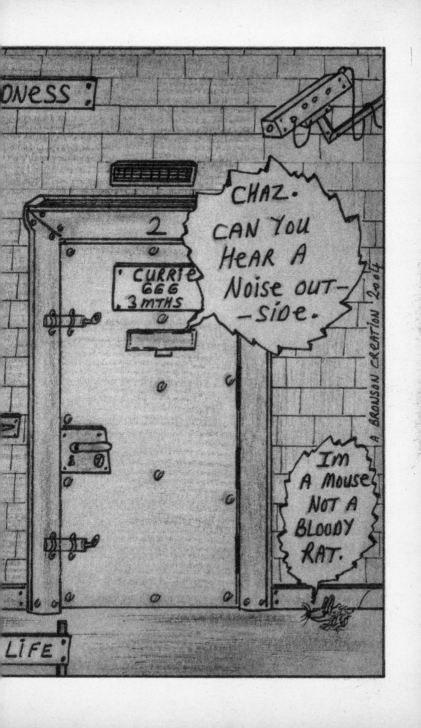

Nothing lasts
Only pain
Love burns up
Hope goes on without you
Dream on
That's all it is
A fucked-up dream
A melting ice cream
A mouldy toffee apple
A candy floss blown away
Growing old
Skin sags
Wrinkles come
Hair falls out
Eyes stop sparkling
Bums and tits sag
Double chins
Beer bellies
Stretch marks of life
Deep creased frowns
Ugly people don't suffer
They were never pretty
They only know how to be ugly
Lucky bastards
Only the pretty ones cry with age
The vain fuckers
I love it
Don't you?
When they look in the mirror, they want to scream
One day they are pretty

The next they are ugly
You are now in the mirror again
Look at the crow's feet
You're on your way
Age is turning you ugly
The sexy ones are crying
You're no longer sexy
You're fucking ugly
Go and cut the grass
Sleep in the spare room
Stop looking in my direction
Stop breathing in my space
Here's ten grand
Go and visit a surgeon
A plastic job
Get it sorted ... or move out
Neck looks like an ostriche's
Feet smell
Breath smells
Dick shrinks
Erections disappear
Sleep a lot
Fart a lot
Snore a lot
You're dead meat
It's over
Plastic surgery
Plastic people
You become false
A puppet

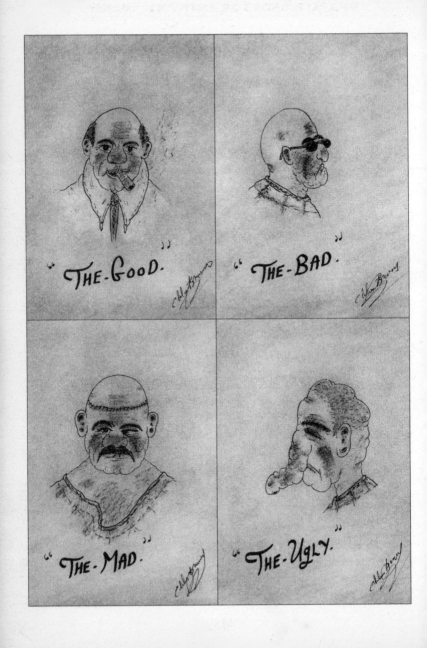

So who's pulling your strings?
We all know it's a wig
False tits, too
False teeth as well
You're no longer who you were
You're somebody else
You have lost your way
You daft bastard
Who are you fooling?
Yourself?
You false prat
What a waste of money
What a waste of life
Look in the mirror now
Who are you?
What are you?
You are a joke
A piss-taker
Look into the toilet bowl
The reflection
Take a picture
Have a laugh
'Cos you're giving us one
You give us all a good laugh
It's time you saw the funny side
Wake up
Mae West said it all
Ninety years old when she said,
'It's not the men in my life, it's the life in my men'
I now feel sick

Pass the sick bag
Stop it!
Fucking stop this bus
It's out of control
Who the fuck is driving, Dave Courtney?
That mad fucker
Stop the bus
I'm getting off
It's gonna crash
Jump off
Don't go down this road
It's madness
A freak show
Look at the passengers
Their faces
Their eyes
Look at him over there
He makes the elephant man look pretty
Look at him
Ugly bastard
When you are a freak, it's so easy
You're born ugly
You live ugly
And you die ugly
It's a fact of life
It's easy
It's not so easy to be pretty
Ask Joan Collins
How much longer can she last?
It must be hard

TEL·CURRIE.
CHAZ·BRONSON.
WWW.FREEBRONSON.COM
HA. He. He. He. He. He.
He. HA. HO. He. He. HA. He. HA. He.
So WHO ARe YOU.
GOOD. BAD. MAD OR JUST UGLY..
2005

I say let's all be ugly
Pretend to be beautiful
If we was all ugly
How much easier would life be?
Be proud of ugliness
I salute you
Stand up for our freaks
Those wonderful freaky fuckers
Amazing
Lovely people
A bit scary
A bit spooky
But don't we love 'em all?
Bring back dwarf-throwing
Why did we ever stop it?
It's fun to throw a dwarf
It's what they are there for
What good are they?
All midgets need throwing about
Cheer the world up
Bring it back
Three cheers for our dwarfs
We love 'em
Bring back the bearded lady
And the lizard man
What about the two-headed nun
From Borneo?
I bet the Bat Girl can move in the dark
They are all legends
Icons

Some are myths
They are all magic to me
Bring back the freak shows
Let's have a bloody good laugh

Let's knight the Kray twins
Why not?
They are legends
Ron and Reg are icons
Let's knight Ronnie Biggs
And all the Great Train Robbers
Why not?
Men of history
They stuck it right up the system
Books, TV, plays, movies
They are history-makers
Like Robin Hood
He still lives on
The Sheriff of Nottingham
Who was that?
Who knows his name?
Nobody!
A boring bastard
But Robin was the 'chap'
The guv'nor of the time
His life was fast
Full of excitement
Fearless
We love a villain
Al Capone died years ago

But everyone still remembers him
He was a somebody
A legend
He earned the T-shirt
A mobster of quality
A gangster of style
So who's jealous of it?
Now do you get my drift?
I hope so
Now knight 'em all
Even the dead ones
Don't forget Bonnie Parker and Clyde Barrow
Bonnie and Clyde
Icons
We love 'em to death!

Understand me?
I do hope so
'Cos I don't want to explain again
Why not slip it into my head?
Crawl inside my brain
Blow away my mind
Take me far away
Take me to a rainbow
Fill my heart with colour
Take away the darkness
The blackness of my soul
Blow away the pain
Take me to paradise
Now I'm getting silly

Soft in the nut
My brain's not thinking right
I feel weird
It must have been the fall I had
Knocked me clean out
Senseless and stupid
The long sleep
Dreaming of fairies
Dancing in fields of flowers
Even the animals were dancing
Fucking idiots
I'm nuts
It blew a whole in my crust
It all went red
Blood everywhere
Swimming in crimson
So hard to breathe
My head hurts
Floating into space
To what?
To who?
More isolation
More loneliness
More confusion
Does this shit ever end?
Maybe it's just begun
God help me
I'm not yet born
Not yet started
A re-run

Peaches and cream
I fucking wish
It's figs and dates again
Tons more shit
Piles and piles of shit
Sky high
It cuts out the sky
No more sun
Back to darkness
Back to the beginning
The womb
Return to the unknown
The unborn
Helpless
A seed in the universe
A speck of sand on a beach
Unseen
Blowing through time
Waiting to be free
Free of what?
Free from who?
It's all fucking crazy
Nuts!
It gets madder
More intense
Deeper
Endless
It's fucking for ever
Shit on shit
A pyramid of shit

A turd trail to heaven
Now you're sick
You can fill up a million books
There is not enough pens or paper
Not enough time
You are running out of time
You are writing in time
Soon it's over
You can't write the end
Nobody can
'Cos there is no end chapter
Bin Laden's out there
Bush is on the edge
A power freak
Blair's a puppet
Bush will be pushed
Blair will jump
Bring back Genghis Khan
Let's have a real leader of men
Fearless
A born fighter
Born to be king
A ruler of men
A god
Someone with balls
Not these wimps of today
A dog without a tail
Why cut a dog's tail off?
It's not only cruel
It's fucking wicked!

Evil
Why go fox hunting?
You wicked bastards
A poor little fox
You cruel swines
In fact ... It's pathetic
Grown men chasing a fox
Grow up you prats
Who shoots the rhino?
Who kills the elephant?
Trophy-hunters
You want the ivory
You want the lion's head
Stuffed
On your trophy wall
'Look what I shot'
One to the nut
Between the eyes
You can see the hole
A 30 stone beast
Bang, one shot
All mine
Easy
Fucking cowards
You are a wanker
A nobody
Do it without a rifle
Fight it like a man
Big brave hunter
Wicked bastard

Get a life, you prat
Wake up and die
Stop pretending to be hard
A big gun don't make you tough
Try fighting
Survive as a man
Man to man
In a ring
Fists
Leave our animals alone
Eat them to survive
But why kill them for fun?
What a poxy life
What a great big farce
The world's gone mad
Beyond cure
Ugly
Fucking gruesome
It makes you sick
Sick to your teeth
Sick in your head
Wanna buy some puke?
£3.50 a bag
Roll up ... roll up
Plenty of it
I'm not greedy am I?
I'm not silly either
£3.50 a bag ... pure puke
Whatever happened to humanity?
Love and tenderness

Love thy neighbour
Nowadays, it's let's screw the fuckers
Rip 'em off
Get one over on the daft bastards
Kick them when they are down
In the bollocks
Good and hard
Bleed them dry
Suck them hollow
Burgle them when they are out
Set fire to their cat
Put the dog in the microwave
Dig up the rose beds
Have a laugh
Upset the posh gits
It's all dried up
One big drought
Not one drop of kindness left
Dehydrated
A dried-up prune
Crumbled
Dust to dust
What a way to go
Crawling away in disgust
Killing for fun
Only the strong go on
The weak are pig swill
Eat up and shit back out
Watch the vultures
Ripping away the flesh

Pecking out the eyes
Only the bones remain
The brain is a delicacy
Watch the sewer rats
Some as big as cats
Razor teeth
Razor sharp
Hell on earth
The tunnels of Satan
Rat-infested
Thousand and millions
Rats on rats
Screeching in the dark
I dare you to go down
Without a torch
I dare you
You won't come back
That's for sure
You fucking coward
Get down there
It's where you belong
You are a rat
The biggest rat on the planet
Vermin
Like that slag Rose West
Born to suck away life
Evil bitch
A bitch witch
Like that pervo Gary Glitter
'Wanna be in my gang?'

His gang are a bunch of nonces
Child-abusers
Like that Jonathan King
Paedophiles
Evil sick bastards
Twisted and sick
Beyond a nightmare
Human predators
Bullies of children
Cowards to men
Mice to men
Lions to kids
Fucking scum
Leave our kids alone
You sickos
Pick on someone your own size
Pick on me
Yeah, me!
I dare you
Fucking cowards
What's next?
What comes next?
Tell me?
World War III
Bombs out of space
Destruction
I hope it lands on the religious freaks
Those extremest bastards
Stirring it up
Hate breeders

Believe in my god or die
Some god
They are all the fucking same
Freaks of god
Killing for god
Bombing other religions
Why?
God is God, ain't he?
Peaceful
So why kill each other?
Fucking hypocrites
Two-faced prats
Who gives a flying fuck?
I don't
They are all as bad as one another
Be like me
God is in the heart
Not in a building
A church, a temple or mosque
They are all shit-houses
A building
Bricks and mortar
God is in us all
He isn't no religion
Religion is man-made
It's all fucked-up lies
Exaggerated beyond belief
The Simpsons are more sense
Scooby-fucking-Doo
Yogi Bear

I have more faith in a fish finger
Talking of fish
They do a smashing fish 'n' chips in Broadmoor Asylum
I would kill for their fish 'n' chips
Awesome
Very tasty
Ronnie Kray loved his fish 'n' chips
All the loonies love it
Apart from the vegans
But who are they anyway?
Fucked up in the head
Brain-dead zombies

Talking of brain dead
I wonder how the Yorkshire Ripper is?
My pal Ian Kaye tore his eye out
Sad it wasn't both eyes
He needs blinding, that evil swine
13 women he blew out
Sicko
Hang 'em high
It's the only way
Why keep them alive?
On taxpayers' money
What a waste
All dried up
All washed away
A beached whale
Dying
You can't save it

It's gone too far
No way back
Dig a hole

Ronnie 'The Rocket' O'Sullivan done it again
What a player
What a champ
King of the table
Respect to him
A genius
A one-off
I see Leeds went down
Good ... wankers!
Billy Bremner would turn in his grave
What a fucking disaster
Those footballers get paid too much
Over-paid prats
No heart left in the game
It's all about money now
Greedy fuckers
Sir Stanley Matthews played for peanuts proper
He played with pride
So did Greavsie
So did they all in the old days
'Sportsmen of Honour'
It's all changed now
Life's changed
Even the villians are prats
Selling drugs to kids
Fucking lowlifes

What a nasty planet
God must be depressed
A chronic depressive
How sad is that?
It can't get any worse
Look at that Hungerford massacre
Michael 'Mad Dog' Ryan
What was all that about?
Son of Sam
What about that fat Scotch rat, Thomas Hamilton?
Blowing that school class away
The Dunblane massacre
Does it get any worse than that?
Or Ian Huntley or Ian Brady
Now where's the religion?
I'm sick of reading about nonce priests
Bending the choir boys over the altar
Wake up!
It's how the world is ... sick
AIDS is spreading
Millions have now got it
Babies are now born with it
Is that sad or what?
Dying before they are born
Some are born herion addicts
Can you believe that?
Cold turkey before their eyes open
It's wicked
It's cruel
It's against humanity

Where's all the love?
All dried up

Watch the old man in a London street
Homeless
Jobless
Penniless
Sleeping in a box
Cardboard
He's got TB
He's got terrible piles
Cancer, too
He cries a lot
In pain
He shakes
DTs
Parkinson's Disease
Hurry up and take me, it lingers on
A tramp in the night
A piss-head
A walking fucking disease
A human germ
He ended up under a train
His way out
Nobody missed him
No fucker knew him
The prick lost himself
He died years ago
He forgot to bury himself
They burnt him

Nobody came
He left nothing
Not even a name
A nobody
What a fucking life ... it stinks

I watched the tart work
Always on the same corner
Always with the big black pimp
He had a gold tooth
A big fur coat
Dripping with gold
A Rolex watch
He had a red Porsche
Crocodile shoes
A gold cigarette case
A true live pimp
Fucking parasite
She was once so pretty
Full of smiles
Beautiful teeth
With big blue shiny eyes
Now look
27 years old
Looks 50
Old and haggard
Smelly and scabby
VD, syphilis
She's got it all
Scabies, too

She sucks her way to an early grave
Teeth rotten
The smack has gone to work
It's destroying her
All for a cock
What a disaster
Somebody shot that pimp
Could be your sister next
Could be your mum
Pray it's not
You'd better believe it
It's in your face
Your nextdoor neighbour
That pervo at the end of your street
Watching you

I see that movie *The Green Mile*
How fucking green was that?
Death row
The chair
Sizzle the brain big time
Great movie
Lots of feeling and emotion
Made me choked up
That's rare for me
Titanic
That went down well!
Gladiators?
They couldn't punch their way out of a bag
Fucking silly actors

I'll fight that Russell Crowe
With one hand behind my back
I'll show him what a gladiator is
Fucking idiot
Wake up and smell the shit
It's knee deep
I lay awake laughing
I laugh so much it hurts
My ribs are rattling
They rush me
They restrain me
I'm put in a straitjacket
Tightly
Very tight
It's hard to breathe
It's difficult to move
I need to scratch my nose
I can't
I need to shit
I need to wake up
To awake in a nice dream
All this shit is suffocating me
It's blinding my vision
I'm old
Worn out
Lost in time
But I'm still in this sewer
The rats have become friendly
I'm no longer afraid
Even death would be a blessing

A hole in my head a result
It can't go on much more
The birdman is losing the plot
The poet from hell has finally drowned

All dried up ...

Charlie Bronson, 2004

Time Is the Serpent

So we float away on another day
Feet laden with light hope
Time bears talons like bird of prey to feast on our fears
Fear of time itself, the serpent that welcomes death to the
shell
The serpent breathes cold on your cheek
The cunning is in the gentle
Sweeping up the fragments of our shredded souls, we
call this experience

To pick the solitary ripe fruit from decaying fragments,
we call this learning
To be carved by the warrior wind
Innocence torn from feeble flesh
Mind poisoned by twisted tongues
Blood is the strength of us, love is the leech
The serpent hisses on every tick
He crawls through the crack in your shell
He can wait, he will wait
For unlike us, he is eternal.

Tel Currie

Lest We Forget

Lest we forget the fallen ones; our freedom their dying
breath
Resurrection of all our hopes rose from their own death
Think not of them as history, for the present owes them deep
Far from home they came to rest, far from where their
widows weep
For a painful yard of land they fell, each one somebody's son
For a cause they gave their lives, before it had begun

Lest we forget the living, whose ears still hear the blast
For they shall live each new day, with souls at half mast
Medals upon their chest they wear for those they left
behind
A tear shed as their brothers in battle go marching
through their minds
We must protect the dove of peace they won so fragile in
their hands
For we know upon its death comes another destruction
of the land

Lest we forget where they fell, The Somme, Alamein and
Verdun, Rangoon, Gallipoli, Normandy and Arnhem to
the land of the rising sun
Lest we forget those buried on a foreign shore
And lest we forget the epitaph; their name liveth for
ever more.

Tel Currie

Pain

Pain, pain rapist of man
Take your salt from my open wounds
Rusty sword twist in my soul
Torture of naked spirit
Weeping heart of screaming pain
Invade and enter me again

Demonic eye will spear me now
Of graveyard breath you reek
Parasite of my mind's walls
Cancer of my soul
Unhand my heart I have to live
Come to me sleep that dulls the pain
Then raped by you another day

Tel Currie

Key Dates

13 December 1922 – Frankie Fraser born
8 August 1929 – Ronnie Biggs born
27 July 1930 – Eric Mason born
7 September 1931 – Bruce Reynolds born
5 March 1932 – Freddie Foreman born
24 October 1933 – Kray twins born
18 January 1934 – Charlie Richardson born
29 February 1936 – Eddie Richardson born
11 March 1936 – Roy Shaw born
2 November 1937 – Joey Pyle born
25 December 1938 – Chris Lambrianou born
6 March 1943 – Cliff Field born
23 February 1944 – Wilf Pine born
15 April 1947 – Tony Lambrianou born
9 July 1947 – Billy Hill takes over London's underworld in 'The Battle That Never Was'
24 May 1947 – Kenneth Noye born
6 June 1948 – 'Gypsy' Johnny Frankham born

9 April 1949 – Lenny McLean born

6 December 1951 – Michael Peterson – aka Charles Bronson – born

11 August 1955 – Jack 'Spot' and Albert Dimes fight it out in Soho in 'The Battle That Never Was' or 'The Battle of Frith Street'

2 May 1956 – Jack 'Spot' slashed by 'Mad' Frankie Fraser, 'Ginger' Dennis and others

25 June 1956 – The murder of Tommy Smithson

3 March 1958 – Cass Pennant born

21 July 1958 – Stellakis Stylianou – AKA Stilks – born

14 December 1958 – Ronnie Marwood kills PC Summers

17 February 1959 – Dave Courtney born

1 March 1959 – Carlton Leach born

8 May 1959 – Ronnie Marwood hanged for the stabbing of PC Summers; the Nash brothers lay wreaths

7 February 1960 – The Pen Club shootings; Selwyn Cooney dies and Jimmy Nash, Joey Pyle and John Read are arrested

8 August 1963 – The Great Train Robbery

15 April 1964 – The Great Train Robbers sentenced to up to 30 years

20 April 1965 – Tommy 'Ginger' Marks shot dead by Freddie Foreman; he was never seen again

20 April 1965 – Reggie Kray and Frances Shea are married

8 July 1965 – Ronnie Biggs goes over the wall at Wandsworth Prison

24 July 1965 – Former World light-heavyweight champion Freddie Mills found dead in his car in Soho; the official verdict is suicide

7 March 1966 – Dickie Hart is shot dead in 'The Battle of Mr

Smith's'; Eddie Richardson and Frankie Fraser receive gunshot wounds

9 March 1966 – George Cornell shot dead by Ronnie Kray in the Blind Beggar pub

12 August 1966 – Three policemen shot dead by Harry Roberts, John Duddy and John Witney in Shepherd's Bush, West London

12 December 1966 – Frank 'The Mad Axeman' Mitchell sprung from Dartmoor by members of the Kray firm

24 December 1966 – Frank Mitchell shot dead by Freddie Foreman and Alf Gerrard

7 June 1967 – Reggie Kray's wife Frances commits suicide aged 23 years

28 October 1967 – Jack 'The Hat' McVitie stabbed to death by Reggie Kray

8 May 1968 – Ron and Reg Kray arrested at Braithwaite House

8 March 1969 – Ron and Reg Kray get life at the Old Bailey with a 30-year recommendation

7 May 1970 – David Knight, Brother of Ronnie and John Knight, killed

22 April 1971 – Car bomb explodes under the car of Jimmy Tibbs

10 August 1972 – The Wembley Barclays Bank job

March 1973 – Bertie Smalls turns supergrass

4 September 1974 – Alfred 'Italian Tony' Zomparelli murdered in Soho

8 July 1975 – Bernie Silver jailed for the killing of Tommy Smithson nearly 20 years before

1 December 1975 – The first ever unlicensed fight is

contested in Billy Smart's Big Top near Windsor between Donny 'The Bull' Adams and Roy 'Pretty Boy' Shaw;
Roy wins easily in the first round

18 October 1976 – Bernie Silver's sentence quashed

11 September 1978 – The third fight between Roy Shaw and Lenny McLean billed as 'Close Encounter for a Third Time'

17 January 1980 – George Piggott jailed for murder of Tony Zomparelli

23 May 1980 – Charlie Richardson escapes

19 November 1980 – Ronnie Knight cleared of the murder of Tony Zomparelli

18 January 1981 – Charlie Richardson recaptured

24 March 1981 – Ronnie Biggs kidnapped

27 June 1982 – Nicky Gerrard, son of Alf Gerrard, murdered

28 January 1983 – Armed robber David Martin captured

4 April 1983 – The Security Express robbery in Curtain Road, Shoreditch, London, Britain's biggest ever cash robbery

26 November 1983 – The Brinks Mat bullion robbery at Heathrow

26 January 1985 – DC John Fordham killed in Kenny Noye's property

10 June 1985 – John Knight sentenced for 22 years for Security Express robbery

12 July 1987 – Knightsbridge safety deposit box robbery

28 July 1989 – Freddie Foreman forced back to England from Spain

23 April 1990 – Great Train Robber Charlie Wilson murdered at his Spanish villa

3 August 1991 – David Brindle shot dead

17 August 1991 – Arthur Thompson Jnr killed

12 June 1992 – Paul Ferris cleared of Arthur Thompson Jnr's murder

13 March 1993 – Arthur Thompson Snr dies

1 June 1993 – Jimmy Moody shot dead in what is said to be revenge for David Brindle

30 November 1994 – Great Train Robber Buster Edwards commits suicide; he is found hanging in his flower stall lock-up garage

17 March 1995 – Ronnie Kray dies

29 March 1995 – Ronnie Kray's funeral; at the time, this was the biggest funeral London had seen since Sir Winston Churchill's; Reg Kray appoints Dave Courtney to overlook security

6 December 1995 – 'The Range Rover Murders'; Tony Tucker, Patrick Tate and Craig Rolfe found shot dead in a Range Rover near Rettendon, Essex. Jack Whomes and Mickey Steele are later convicted of the murders on the evidence of Darren Nicholls

14 July 1997 – Reg Kray marries Roberta Jones in HMP Maidstone

21 August 1997 – Great Train Robber Roy James dies

28 July 1998 – Lenny McLean dies

4 April 2000 – Charlie Kray dies

19 April 2000 – Charlie Kray's funeral

26 August 2000 – Reg Kray released on compassionate grounds after 32 years in prison

1 October 2000 – Reggie Kray dies

12 October 2000 – Reg Kray's funeral; the funeral is boycotted by many faces because of the arrangements

7 May 2001 – Ronnie Biggs arrives back in Britain, his first time back on home soil for nearly 40 years; he is still in HMP Belmarsh ... WHY?

1 June 2001 – Charlie Bronson marries Saira Rehman in HMP Woodhill

12 August 2002 – Dave Courtney is involved in a near fatal car 'accident'; he survives but suffers horrific injuries

18 September 2002 – Freddie Foreman attacks 'Mad' Frankie Fraser in a Maida Vale café; the attack was revenge for disrespectful things Frank had publicly said about Fred in a book and TV programmes

14 January 2003 – Ronnie Biggs assaulted by prison officers while lying partially paralysed in HMP Belmarsh

25 February 2004 – Tony Lambrianou dies

26 February 2004 – Warriors IV Unlicensed fight show; Tel Currie dedicates the show to Charlie Bronson before his upcoming appeal; there is also a tribute to Tony Lambrianou; Charlie Bronson's artwork along with other memorabilia raises hundreds of pounds for children's charities

11 March 2004 – Tony Lambrianou's funeral

2 April 2004 – Charlie Bronson loses appeal to have life conviction overturned but Lord Justice Rose says, 'I urge the Parole Board to consider a very different man to the one originally sentenced.'

11 June 2004 – Dave Courtney found 'not guilty' of ABH

13 June 2004 – The play *Saira* opens in London; Charlie Bronson appoints a hand-picked team of friends, including Tel Currie, Stilks and Max Iacovou to look after Saira and Sami; the play is a roaring success

6 July 2004 – Charlie Bronson is refused parole

7 July 2004 – Despite the fact Charlie Bronson's visits are all closed and behind bars, a visitor to Wakefield Prison is disgusted to see Ian Huntley, the killer of Holly and Jessica, enjoying a cosy open visit

18 July 2004 – *News of the World* carries a pull-out called 'Britain's Most Evil', containing, in their opinion, the 50 most evil people in the UK. Charlie Bronson is number 38. Despite the fact he has never killed or pulled the trigger, he is considered more evil than Victor Miller, Roy Whiting, Ian Huntley, Peter Sutcliffe, Rose West and Ian Huntley!

18 September 2004 – The launch of the official Free Bronson Campaign and website takes place at Charlie Breaker's pub in London. On this same day Charlie Bronson splits from Saira. It's all over.

March 2005 – Divorce. The Bronsons are history. Charlie gets lots of shit in the press which is very hurtful to him. He's accused by some as being a racist thug. It's all to keep the man in a hole. It's all on www.freebronson.com. One thing's for sure, Charlie may be all 'Good, bad, mad and ugly', but one thing he isn't is a racist.

Nevertheless Charlie wishes Saira 'a good journey.' He freed a bird!

Some men are meant to go it alone. Some need a woman, some don't. Charlie is more than content with his lovely mum Eira and his beautiful sister Loraine.

Oh! And Bertha! Who you may ask ...?

Check it out.

So WHO ARE YOU?
GOOD. BAD. MAD. –
– OR UGLY?
"WHATEVER".... IF YOUR IN –
– THIS BOOK I SALUTE YOU.
YOUR THE DOGS BOLLOCKS.
THE CREAM OF THE CROP.
WE LOVE YA.
(APART FROM THE BAD ONES)..

2004

Recommended Websites

www.freebronson.com - the *only* official Bronson site!

www.royprettyboyshaw.com

www.ronniebiggs.com

www.davecourtney.com

www.gangstervideos.co.uk

www.thekrays.co.uk

www.casspennant.com

www.terryturbo.com

www.crimethroughtime.com

Other Books by Charlie Bronson

The Krays and Me
The Good Prison Guide
Bronson
Birdman Opens His Mind
Insanity
Solitary Fitness

Other Books by Tel Currie

Bouncers with Julian Davies